The Diagrams of
Architecture

Edited by **Mark Garcia**

A John Wiley and Sons Ltd, Publication

Registered office
John Wiley & Sons Ltd, The Atrium, Southern Gate,
Chichester, West Sussex, PO19 8SQ, United Kingdom

For details of our global editorial offices, for customer services and for information about how to apply for permission to reuse the copyright material in this book please see our website at www.wiley.com.

Executive Commissioning Editor: Helen Castle
Project Editor: Miriam Swift
Publishing Assistant: Calver Lezama
Content Editor: Françoise Vaslin

ISBN   978-0-470-51944-8 (hb)
              978-0-470-51945-5 (pb)

Designed by Artmedia, London.
Printed by Everbest, China.

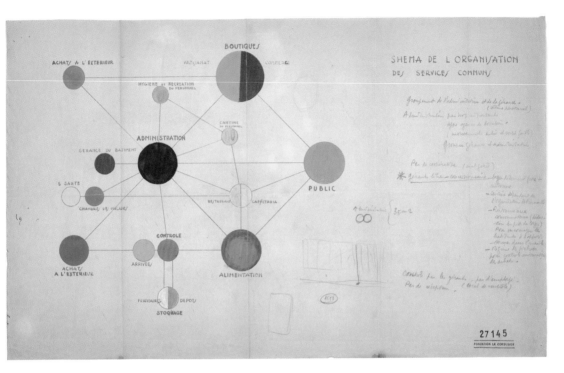

Le Corbusier, Marseille: Unité d'habitation, 1945. Bubble diagram of communal services for the building complex. © FLC/ADAGP, Paris and DACS, London 2008.

Le Corbusier and model showing his use of the Modulor system diagram in a 3-D physical model of a building system, c 1945–53. © Michel Sima/Getty Images.

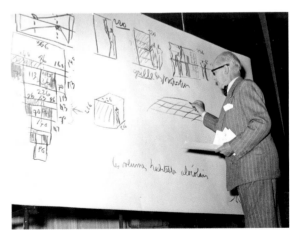

Le Corbusier making a presentation at the Triennale, Milan, 1951. He often lectured on architecture, using and making diagrams on the spot. © FLC/ADAGP, Paris and DACS, London 2008.

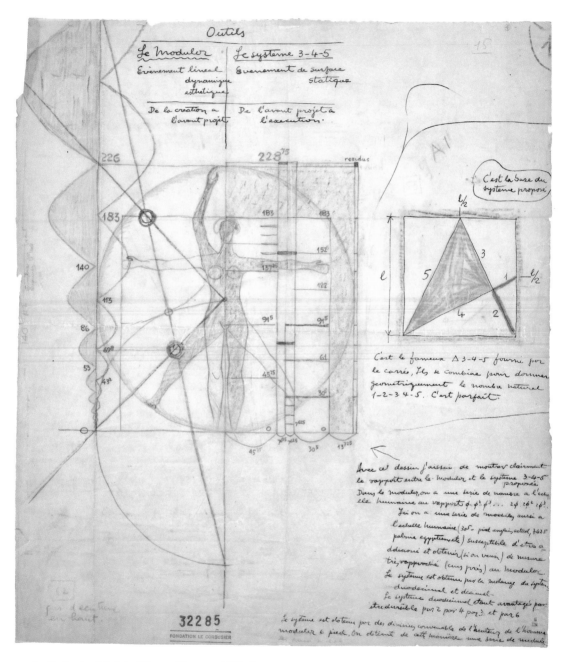

Le Corbusier, Modulor Woman Diagram, 1952. ©
FLC/ADAGP, Paris and DACS, London 2008.

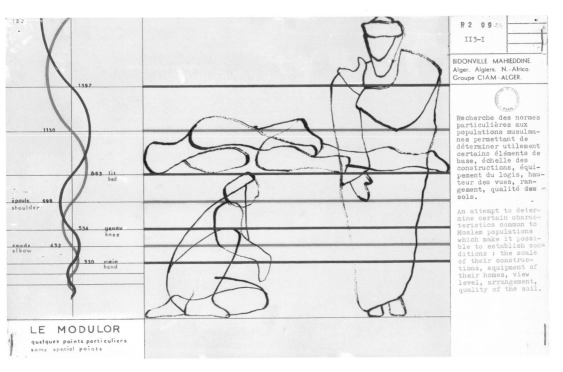

Le Corbusier, Moslem Modulor Diagram, 1955. A page from his study of the shanty town 'Bidonville Mahieddiene' in Algiers for the CIAM conference in Algeria in 1955. The diagram is part of Corbusier's attempt to determine, by extending his Modulor diagram system, the Moslem conditions of space, including (from the text in the image) 'the scale of their construction, equipment of their homes, view level, arrangement, quality of the soil'. © FLC/ADAGP, Paris and DACS, London 2008.

Chandigarh: Palace of Assembly, 1955. The diagrams Le Corbusier included in his enamelled doors for the main entrance to the palace show the path of the sun across the sky in summer and winter (top) and the path of the sun across the sky, relative to the horizon, through 24 hours (top right). Many of Le Corbusier's diagrams were transformed into paintings, sculptures and other artworks. © FLC/ADAGP, Paris and DACS, London 2008.

Introduction
Histories and Theories of the Diagrams of Architecture

Mark Garcia

> Since the mid-20th century, the diagram has taken first place among the techniques and procedures of architectural knowledge, usurping the place of the drawing … the diagram has gained amazing prominence as a leading term in theoretical discourse.
>
> *Gerrit Confurius,* Daidalos, *vol 74, 2000*

> Diagramming is indeed the most important innovation in architecture of the last 10 to 15 years.
>
> *Lars Spuybroek,* The Architecture of Continuity, *2008*

Definitions of the Diagrams of Architecture

A diagram is the spatialisation of a selective abstraction and/or reduction of a concept or phenomenon. In other words, a diagram is the architecture of an idea or entity. Much effort has been spent (particularly since the mid-1980s) in research into the supposed 'powers' and potentials of the architectural diagram, which have been theorised in a succession of short texts, magazines and a small handful of books. Strong claims have repeatedly been made for the ameliorating and emancipating effects of diagrams, and recent architectural theory and practice in this field continues. Today diagrams are valuable and used in seemingly every aspect of architecture. It is surprising then to find that, considering their centrality and ubiquity, there are not more books, more criticism and a more integrated body of research into the link between diagrams, architecture and other related forms of spatial design. While there is a flood of exceptional design (built, unbuilt and unbuildable) and many interesting theoretical contributions to the field, there are some major omissions, biases and undetected problems. It therefore seems timely to revise and readdress this ancient field in the light of recent developments since the late 20th century, to raise some new questions and to introduce some new contributions, ideas and designs into the historical, contemporary and futurological discourses on the architectural diagram.

Diagrams in architecture are as old as architecture itself. Some of the earliest prehistoric artefacts: Stonehenge in England,[1] the diagram of the town of Konya in Turkey, dated to around 6200 BC, and ancient Amerindian petroglyph diagrams carved into rock, are diagrams of space and place. Even a cursory glance through Michael Friendly's[2] historical and visual survey of diagrams and visualisations indicates that this is a complex field that overlaps various paradigms of knowledge and enquiry. This has resulted in diverse definitions of the diagram and, consequently, very different conceptualisations of its properties, function and use. These differences are also apparent in the way diagrams are

Rock diagram, artist and date unknown. This petroglyph is a diagram of the relations between the local land and its animal and human inhabitants. Associated with Nez Perce ancient Native American Indians, c 2500 BC. © Courtesy of the Bureau of Land Management, Snake River District, Idaho, USA. Photo Barry Rose, 1991.

described and valued in relation to architecture and spatial design, and with respect to questions of validity, truth status, their ontological standing as both process and objects, and as mental and material phenomena. Much new research is being undertaken into how the design of diagrams relates to their value and utility as philosophical, practical and aesthetic phenomena.[3] As Alan Blackwell and Yuri Engelhardt's 'A Meta-Taxonomy for Diagram Research'[4] indicates, the field is a fragmented mix of disciplines, schools of thought and often disjointed research projects. It also suggests many of the ways in which architecture and spatial design have, will and could engage with this important field of multidisciplinary visual and spatial practice and knowledge. Before examining the present or speculating on the future, it is worth considering the specific history of diagrams in architecture.

The design and use of diagrams in architectural texts and treatises was a display of authority and qualification to design, build and/or theorise architecture. Diagrams demonstrated that an architect or writer had the necessary skills and knowledge. Diagrams related to architecture, and to other subjects relating to architecture, were therefore a staple of many architectural treatises as far back as Vitruvius, whose *De Architectura*, or 'Ten Books on Architecture' (c 25 BC), included 9 or 10 accompanying images that (in most cases) were basic geometric diagrams.[5] Vitruvius's text touches on topics in which diagrams are important. These include: astronomy, astrology, geology, physics, anatomy, hydrology, optics, perspective, entarsis, colour, music, acoustics, mathematics, painting, sculpture, geometry, meteorology, engineering, mechanics, armaments and ballistics. Since Vitruvius, the history of the education of the architect (both in and outside the Western tradition), has at different moments up to the present included at least some knowledge of (among other subjects) theology and scripture, mathematics, geometry, philosophy and politics, and later the principles and practices of the arts (drawing, painting, sculpture). Skill and knowledge in these subjects

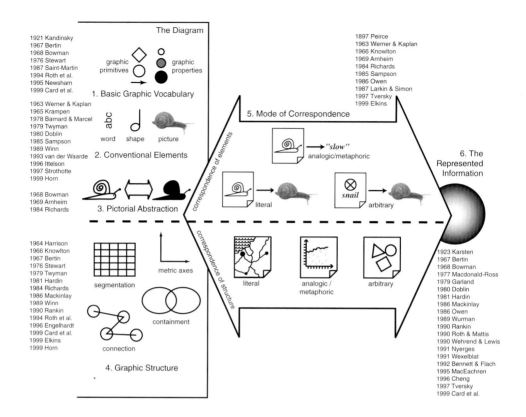

The Diagram

1921 Kandinsky
1967 Bertin
1968 Bowman
1976 Stewart
1987 Saint-Martin
1994 Roth et al.
1995 Newsham
1999 Card et al.

graphic primitives — graphic properties

1. Basic Graphic Vocabulary

1963 Werner & Kaplan
1965 Krampen
1978 Barnard & Marcel
1979 Twyman
1980 Doblin
1985 Sampson
1989 Winn
1993 van der Waarde
1996 Ittelson
1997 Strothotte
1999 Horn

word   shape   picture

2. Conventional Elements

1968 Bowman
1969 Arnheim
1984 Richards

3. Pictorial Abstraction

1897 Peirce
1963 Werner & Kaplan
1966 Knowlton
1969 Arnheim
1984 Richards
1985 Sampson
1986 Owen
1987 Larkin & Simon
1997 Tversky
1999 Elkins

5. Mode of Correspondence

correspondence of elements

"slow"
analogic/metaphoric

literal

snail
arbitrary

6. The Represented Information

correspondence of structure

1964 Harrison
1966 Knowlton
1967 Bertin
1976 Stewart
1979 Twyman
1981 Hardin
1984 Richards
1986 Mackinlay
1989 Winn
1990 Rankin
1994 Roth et al.
1996 Engelhardt
1999 Card et al.
1999 Elkins
1999 Horn

segmentation

metric axes

literal   analogic / metaphoric   arbitrary

containment

connection

4. Graphic Structure

1923 Karsten
1967 Bertin
1968 Bowman
1977 Macdonald-Ross
1979 Garland
1980 Doblin
1981 Hardin
1986 Mackinlay
1986 Owen
1989 Wurman
1990 Rankin
1990 Roth & Mattis
1990 Wehrend & Lewis
1991 Nyerges
1991 Wexelblat
1992 Bennett & Flach
1995 MacEachren
1996 Cheng
1997 Tversky
1999 Card et al.

(particularly since the Renaissance) signalled the architect or architectural theorist's abilities in, and/or comprehension of, classical designo and decorum, reason and order. Some of the diagrams from other disciplines and domains were inevitably transferred into architectural designs, built works, theories and texts. However, due to their perishable and sometimes (deliberately) esoteric, exclusive, inscrutable nature, many of the diagrams created in architectural contexts have not survived, defy interpretation or though intended and operating as such, do not appear to be diagrams.

Leaving aside some important diagrammatic histories of other disciplines related to ancient and classical architecture, it was, remarkably, only in the 20th century that significant texts of architecture theory on the specific subject of the diagram appeared. Only in the 1980s and 1990s did full-scale books emerge with the architectural diagram as their main subject[6] or the word 'diagram' in their title. Even Le Corbusier's chapter 'Truth From Diagrams' in *La Ville Radieuse* (1933) included only basic diagrams related to geoplanetary solar paths and urban zoning. Though many of the diagrams included in his book address the various patterns and dimensions of the space and life cycles of humans, (labour, leisure, politics, technology, transport, agricultural regions and environment etc), Le Corbusier wastes few words on the topic of diagrams in architecture itself, though he himself was a prolific, significant and original diagram architect and designer. It was only in 2005 that the first book devoted to the diagrammatic presentation of architectural precedents (admittedly of

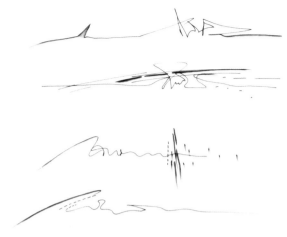

Zaha Hadid, Zollhof 3 Media Park, Dusseldorf, 1989–93.
Freehand diagrams. © Courtesy of Zaha Hadid Architects.

and metaphysical status. The diagram itself has been variously described as process, product, pattern, object, structure, visualisation, spatialisation, concept, idea, event, flow, detail, primary generator, recording, intuition, tool, trace, proposition, solution, conclusion, agent/agency, occasion, formula, heuristic, mnemonic, interface, vehicle, vessel, potential and force. Metaphysically and ontologically it has been described as both real and ideal, objective and subjective, reductive and generative, type and token, emancipatory and oppressive, destructive and ameliorative, social and inhuman, personal and impersonal, material and immaterial, form and formless.[31] It has also been defined through its method of creation, as the natural product or partner of the imagination and intuition, and incidentally or accidentally as a side effect or waste product[32] of the design process. Epistemologically, diagrams have been recommended as useful ways of engaging and researching almost every different kind of architectural type of truth, thinking and reasoning, for skill- and experience-building and for the cognitive pursuit of a variety of aesthetic, ethical, scientific, theoretical and practical modes of architectural enquiry and knowledge.

Some Problems, Criticisms and Gaps in Architectural Diagrams Research
The plethora and proliferation of theories about the architectural diagram has raised some interesting new criticisms of the field, and has opened up a number of conspicuous gaps. Part of the problem with the current state of diagrams has to do with how they have been understood historically and their propensity to resist certain forms of interpretation.

They can be so perceptually, subjectively and contextually contingent[33] and specific as to render them ephemeral and interpretively intractable, except for brief periods, even to their makers. Diagrams (like process-based and conceptual works of art and architecture) can be highly obscure, esoteric and personal, and made, used and experienced in such uncertain mental states, contexts and conditions that they can be considered, in Umberto Eco's sense, polyguous, 'open works' of sorts.[34]

Cedric Price, diagram and sketch for Generator, White Oak,
Florida, 1976–9. Fonds Cedric Price, Collection Centre Canadien
d'Architecture/Canadian Centre for Architecture, Montreal. © CCA.

Though they are often fundamental to works of architecture, diagrams can remain latent, hidden and even deliberately disguised[35] or decorated, making it difficult to decipher and interpret them, and appreciate their effects and functions in architecture. Occasionally, as with an indexical type of diagram, they can be epiphenomenal and made (sometimes under automatist and generative conditions whereby the author or authorship is diffused) outside the full control, intention or understanding of the maker.

The classical theorisation of architectural and art-historical drawings through traditional Western, object-based (as opposed to process-based and conceptual art) aesthetic discourses interpreted, valued and raised the drawing above the diagram, ignoring the latter's possible artful or aesthetic possibilities. The diagram was framed as a primitive 'sketch' or trivial 'process'-related artefact, a kind of proto- or ersatz drawing. But this is to confuse the sketch-drawing with the sketch-diagram. The sketch-diagram, unlike the sketch-drawing does not have to be construed primarily in relation to the arts or to the drawing and the model. It can be described with its own history and in relation to subjects and domains that extend beyond arts-based traditions, conventions of the media and modes of design.[36]

limitations. The most serious omissions, biases and gaps in existing writings that critique and reinterpret architectural diagrams, or texts about them, tend to replicate the confused, fragmented field of diagram research overall. They suffer from historical myopia and inattention to the futurological trajectories of diagram research in other fields. Because of the evolving and expanding definitions and research into the various mutations and adaptations of the diagram in other (often highly specific) domains and disciplines, much of the criticism in extant writings on the diagram in architecture presents an insular, superficial, biased, unrepresentative and anachronistic concept of the forefront and futures of the diagram beyond the limits of architecture. More specifically, criticisms of the diagram tend to be similar and they target similar issues – for example, that diagrams:

- lack the aesthetic qualities of drawings or are not art;[43]

- have negative and undesirable aspects because of their association with formalism, reduction, abstraction and simplicity;[44]

- deal poorly with their multisensory and phenomenological content (or that of a design or building related to a diagram);[45]

- are ideological, rhetorical and polemical though they are claimed to be neutral or unrelated to politics;[46]

- are not logically or clearly connected in a linear and deterministic or methodologically transparent way to the resulting final building they are associated with;[47]

- are scaled up or down erroneously and used in ways that confuse the map with the territory or are pointlessly used to determine architecture or a space with datascapes and indexes;[48]

- are impoverished in the digital realm because digital tools and methods make the ease of generating multiple and successive iterations of diagrams potentially thoughtless;[49]

- have not been used to engage fully with society and social issues;[50]

- have not been used to explore architecture's full multidisciplinary potentials, and connections and the negative consequences of extending these to domains outside architecture;[51] nor have the dangers and ease of erroneous overextensions of architectural diagrams in to areas outside architecture or architectural expertise been adequately documented.

A further analysis of the field also suggests a number of other, new criticisms of architectural diagrams and texts about them. The most significant are that historical and theoretical (and some design) research into diagrams in architecture:

- is lacking any explicit textual, theoretical engagement with some closely related spatial design disciplines (such as interior design, landscape design, architectural engineering) as well as with significant and relevant fields closely related to architecture (such as interactive architecture, digitally designed architecture, parametric architecture and new and emerging architectural technologies);

- does not engage with more general, important and recent diagram theory and research (such as is found in the work of Michael Friendly,[52] Alan Blackwell, M Anderson et al[53] and Frederik Stjernfelt);[54]

- does not specifically address the recent, emerging impacts of new technologies and the computer (such as interactive systems, parametric design, advanced design and construction software – or example, the parametric design softwares developed by MVRDV and Gehry Technologies – complex digital city models, the micro-scale and nano-, femto- and pico-technologies, new remote sensing/control/mapping technologies and others);

- needs a robust, fundamental taxonomy (or meta-taxonomy) or visual chronology, encyclopaedia or other exhaustive, international, historical survey of diagrams;

- lacks any survey of sceptical, negative criticisms – the overwhelmingly positive theory does not include any multicase, in-depth or recent research on the use of architectural diagrams for exclusion, oppression, deception, obfuscation, propaganda, manipulation and destruction;[55] architecture as a domain seems unaware of the more fundamental, non-architectural theories of the more general impossibilities,[56] imprecisions, limitations, weaknesses and threats of the diagram,[57] though other disciplines, such as cartography, are;[58]

- is devoid of a sufficiently multicultural and international account of architectural diagrams – diagrams and diagrammatic architecture exist in other cultures, as shown in Aborigine,[59] Chinese and other Asian geomantic diagrams (for example, as mandalas, feng shui diagrams, etc), but these are largely ignored or marginalised in the contemporary discourse on the diagram;

- in general, architecture (unlike some other disciplinary domains) lacks any kind of clear, strategic, discipline-wide research programme or any well-articulated or researched account of the possible futures of diagrams in architecture.

9   A recent visual survey, which also comes close is B Ferrater and C Ferrater, *Synchronizing Geometry: Landscape Architecture & Construction/Ideographic Resources*, Actar (Barcelona), 2006, pp 1–47, but it is limited to a historical and structural survey of the diagram in 20th-century architecture and architectural engineering.

10 Paul Emmon's research into bubble diagrams and networks (P Emmons, 'Embodying Networks: Bubble Diagrams and the Image of Modern Organicism', *Journal of Architecture*, vol 11 no 4, pp 441–46), describes the historical, scientific and religious evolution of bubble diagrams, network diagrams and such abstract diagrams as chains, stairs and trees in architecture.

11 Such as *OASE: Diagrams* (Rotterdam), no 48, 1998, Wouter Deen, Udo Garritzman and Like Bijlsmer (eds); Ben van Berkel and Caroline Bos (eds), *ANY: Diagram Work* (New York), no 23', 1998, pp14–57; *Daidalos: Diagrammania* (Berlin), no 74, January 2000, pp 6–79; *Fisuras: Diagramas* (Madrid), vol 12, July 2002; *Lotus International: Diagrams*, no 127, June 2006, pp 4–129; *Architectural Review*, January 2006.

12 The critical anthology of D Cosgrove (ed), *Mappings*, Reaktion (London),1999; K Harmon, *You Are Here: Personal Geographies and Other Maps of the Imagination*, Princeton Architectural Press, (New York), 2003; and J Abrams and P Hall (eds), *Elsewhere/Mapping: Mapping New Cartographies of Networks and Territories*, University of Minnesota Design Institute (Minneapolis, MN), 2006, include useful but fragmented or narrowly focused visual surveys.

13 B Lootsma, 'The Diagram Debate', in *Fisuras: Diagramas* (Madrid), no 12.5, July 2002, pp 146–176.

14 In Eisenman's assessment, Deleuze interprets the diagrams as 'no longer an auditory or visual archive, but a map, a cartography that is coextensive with the whole social field. It is an abstract machine,' P Eisenman, 'Diagram: An Original Scene of Writing', in P Eisenman (introduction by RE Somol), *Peter Eisenman: Diagram Diaries*, Thames & Hudson (London), 1999, p 30.

15 P Aurelli and G Mastrigli in their article 'Architecture After the Diagram'. In *Lotus International, Diagrams*, 127, 2006, pp 96–105, date the rise of diagrammatic city planning to the late 1940s but the field has some earlier precedents, for example, the earliest cadastral plan, produced in 1427 was to assess property ownership and for the collection of taxes in Florence.

16 J Krauss, 'Information at a Glance: On the History of the Diagram', *OASE* (Rotterdam), no 48, 2000 pp 3–29.

17 See the Periodic Table of diagrams at www.visual-literacy.org/periodic_table/periodic_table.html and the Wikipedia entry for diagrams http://en.wikipedia.org/wiki/Diagram. Both provide an indication of the general and highly specific types of extant diagrams currently available.

18 Rowan Wilken elaborates a more extensive interpretation of the etymology of the diagram, drawing on Jacques Derrida. See R Wilken, Diagrammatology, http://www.electronicbookreview.com/thread/electropoetics/intermingled (accessed 29 January 2009).

19 The cartoon is a diagrammatic in so far as it is reductive and abstracting. The stereotype and the caricature are, in this sense, also diagrammatic characterisation. OMA has reduced its buildings to silhouetted cartoon characters in their book *Content* (2003), recognising the cartoon's iconic powers. Neurath and Clendining used cartoons and FAT, Wes Jones and Nigel Coates still use cartoons in their architectural designs.

20 See the chapter 'Small Outline of a Theory of the Sketch' in F Stjernfelt, *Diagrammatology: An Investigation on the Borderlines of Phenomenology, Ontology, and Semiotics*, Kluwer (Dordrecht) 2007.

21 Arthur Miller claims that diagrams and visualisations in the arts and sciences played a 'causal role in scientific creativity', that these are 'usually essential for scientific advance', and can generate 'scientific theories that can carry truth value' (pp 320–1), and that 'a higher plateau in problem solving is attained once visual representations are offered' (p 399), in A Miller, *Insights of Genius: Imagery and Creativity in Science and Art*, MIT Press (Cambridge, MA), 2000, pp 321–326.

22 G Deleuze, *Foucault*, University of Minneapolis Press (Minneapolis, MN), 1988.

23 For Deleuze's philosophy of the diagram see G Deleuze, 'The Diagram' in Constantin Boundas (ed), *The Deleuze Reader*, trans Constantin Boundas and Jacqueline Code, Columbia University Press (New York), 1993.

24 See C Buci-Glucksman, 'On the Diagram in Art', *ANY: Diagram Work* (New York), no 23, 1998, pp34–6 and P Ednie-Brown, 'The Texture of Diagrams: Reasonings on Greg Lynn and Francis Bacon', *Daidalos: Diagrammania* (Berlin), no 74, January 2000, pp 72–9.

25 S Cassara (ed), *Peter Eisenman: Feints*, Skira (Milan), 2006, pp 19–27.

26 A Vidler, 'What is a Diagram Anyway?' in S Cassara (ed), *Peter Eisenman: Feints*, Skira (Milan), 2006, 19–27.

27   RE Somol, 'Dummy text, or the Diagrammatic Basis of Contemporary Architecture', P Eisenman, *Diagram Diaries*, p 7.

28   P Ednie-Brown, 'The Texture of Diagrams: Reasonings on Greg Lynn and Francis Bacon', *Daidalos*: *Diagrammania* (Berlin), no 74, January 2000, pp 72–9.

29   The 'diagrammatic intention' or the state of mind which intends to experience the world in, through or as diagrams is, as Stjernfelt notes, 'in itself an interpretant of a symbol' and therefore the antecedent condition of its object, forming the equivalent of a Kantian 'schema' and as such part of its (phenomenological) being (F Stjernfelt, *Diagrammatology*, Springer Verlag (Dordrecht), 2007 p 102). For a more detailed discussion of intentional diagrammatic perception and the use of an analytical and experiential use of diagrams see the chapter titled 'Into The Picture' in this volume.

30   Importantly, Ben van Berkel from UN Studio writes that diagrams can be defined by how they are used, namely that anything can become a diagram if it is used as a diagram. In this case his example is his use of the 'Manimal' (portrait), a hybrid, composite face of a man, an ape and a snake, as a 'diagram' in his interview, in 'Between Ideogram and Image-Diagram', *OASE*: *Diagrams* (Rotterdam), no 48, 1998, pp 63–71.

31   Krauss and Bois discuss in R Krauss and YA Bois, *Formless: A User's Guide*, Zone (New York), 1997, Warhol's use of the diagram in his 'Dance Diagram' of 1962 (p 99) and Lacan's 'L-Schema' diagram (p 91) in the context of the discourse of the formless in art. RE Somol, 'Dummy Text, or the Diagrammatic Basis of Contemporary Architecture', P Eisenman, *Diagram Diaries*, pp 6–25, also refers to the 'informal' nature of the diagram.

32   For some, like Jacques Herzog, quoted in the leaflet to accompany the exhibition 'Herzog & de Meuron: An Exhibition' at Tate Modern, London, in 2005, they are part of 'the waste products of a thought process'; quoted in Sheena Wagstaff, 'Herzog & de Meuron: An Exhibition', exhibition leaflet, 2005, unpaginated.

33   Perception is itself diagrammatic in the sense that multisensory experiences are the result of disparate sensory impressions; each is an abstract, fragmented representation of the perceived phenomenon, which are then combined in the brain. The Gutenberg Diagram is the diagram that describes the pattern traced by the eyes when the focus is aimed at evenly organised, similar visual information. Research from brain and cognitive sciences (see C Ware, *Information Visualisation: Perception for Design*, Elsevier (San Francisco) 2004, and B Roska and F Werblin, 'Vertical interactions Across Ten Parallel, Stacked Representations in the Mammalian Retina', *Nature*, 410.6828, 29 March 2001, pp 583–87) shows that the brain processes visual input from the eyes into a series of between 10 and 12 different, specific, simpler and more abstract versions of the overall impression and then recombines them into a single conscious sense impression. See also the chapters 'Christ Levitating and Two Vanishing Squares' and 'Into The Picture', both in F Stjernfelt, *Diagrammatology*, Springer Verlag (Dordrecht), 2007, for an important best account of diagrammatic visuality. Though this is limited to the contexts of art, the spatial dimensions could easily be extended to the perception of architecture and other designed space.

34   U Eco, *Open Works*, Hutchinson Radius (London), 1989.

35   For example, the various geometrical diagrams developed by Brunelleschi in the 15th century. These form the methodological and spatial basis for paintings, drawings and sculptures that use linear, geometric perspective and projection. Diagrams operate in this way in skeagraphy, chorography and in the digital design and parametric control points, grids, numerical menus and tables and other geometrical, process or effect-control and interfacing instruments and apparatus of design software.

36   For more on this distinction see the chapter 'Small outline of a theory of the sketch', in F Stjernfelt, *Diagrammatology*, Springer Verlag (Dordrecht), 2007, pp 321–26.

37   Anthony Blunt, *Artistic Theory in Italy, 1450–1660*, Oxford University Press (Oxford), [1940] 1985, p 49.

38   The design methods and methodology movement (of which Bruce Archer, John Zeisel, Brian Lawson, John Chris Jones and Nigel Cross are the most significant examples) of the 1960s and 1970s favoured the diagram for its associations with scientific clarity, AI studies and computational, cybernetic systematicity. Christopher Alexander's early work on the diagram and its relations to pattern was clearly influenced by this movement. This has now been supplemented/superseded by more mixed methods and methodologies from the social sciences, arts and humanities.

39   Some examples are the deployment and combination of different, multiple graphic systems of

icons and symbols, textual or other forms of annotations, arrows, axes of factors and variables, and discrete, specific notational systems.

40   P Eisenman, *Diagram Diaries*, Thames & Hudson (London), 1999, pp 23–4.

41   The 'Notation' in art exhibition at the KMC in Karlsruhe, Berlin, September–November 2008 (and the accompanying exhibition catalogue, *Notation: Kalkül und Form in den Künst*, Dieter Appelt, Hubertus von Amelunxen and Peter Weibel (eds), Berlin, 2008), is a precedent.

42   Such as *OASE: Diagrams* (Rotterdam), no 48, 1998, Wouter Deen and Udo Garritzman and L Bijlsmer (eds); *ANY: Diagram Work* (New York), no 23, 1998, pp 14–57; *Daidalos: Diagrammania*, (Berlin), no 74, 1999 (January 2000), pp 6–79; *Fisuras: Diagramas* (Madrid), vol 12.5, July 2002; *Lotus International: Diagrams* (Milan), no 127, June 2006, pp 4–129; *Architectural Review*, (London), January 2006.

43   See for example C Buci-Glucksman, 'On the Diagram in Art', *ANY: Diagram Works* (New York), no 23, 1998, pp34–6 and P Ednie-Brown, 'The Texture of Diagrams: Reasonings on Greg Lynn and Francis Bacon', *Daidalos: Diagrammania* (Berlin), no 74, January 2000, pp 72–9.

44   Reiser + Umemoto, *Atlas of Novel Tectonics*, Princeton University Press (Princeton, NJ), 2006.

45   A history of this critique and of others such as abstraction, reductivism, simplicity, minimalism, universalism, essentialism in the diagram and diagram architecture can be found in A Vidler, 'Diagrams of Diagrams: Architectural Abstraction and Modern Representation', *Representations*, (Berkeley, CA), no 72, Autumn 2000, pp 1–20; P Aurelli and G Mastrigli, 'Architecture after the Diagram', *Lotus International: Diagrams* (Milan), no 127, June 2006, pp 4–129. See also Reiser + Umemoto, *Atlas of Novel Tectonics*.

46   H Pai, *The Portfolio and the Diagram*, MIT Press (Cambridge, MA), 2002, and B Lootsma, 'The Diagram Debate', *Fisuras: Diagramas* (Madrid), no 12.5, July 2002, pp 146–79.

47   Greg Lynn, 'Forms of Expression: The Protofunctional Potential of Diagrams in Architectural Design', *El Croquis* (Barcelona), vol 72 no 1, 1995, p 18 and B Lootsma, 'The Diagram Debate', pp 146–79.

48   Reiser + Umemoto, *Atlas of Novel Tectonics*.

49   A Vidler, 'What is a Diagram Anyway?' in S Cassara (ed), *Peter Eisenman: Feints*, Skira (Milan), 2006 pp 19–27.

50   DA Barber, 'Militant Architecture', in J Rendell, J Hill et al, *Critical Architecture*, Routledge, 2007, pp 57–66, and Robert Somol and Sarah Whiting, 'Notes Around the Doppler Effect and Other Moods of Modernism', in Michael Osman, Adam Ruedig, Matthew Seidel and Lisa Tilney (eds), *Mining Autonomy*, special issue of *Perspecta* (Cambridge, MA), no 33, 2002, pp 72–7.

51   D Barber, 'Militant Architecture', pp 57–66.

52   The York University project is a major multidisciplinary research project in this domain, particularly because of its emphasis on the visual/designed aspects of the field. See http://www.math.yorku.ca/SCS/Gallery/milestone/ (accessed 29 January 2009).

53   AF Blackwell and Y Engelhardt, 'A Meta-Taxonomy for Diagram Research', in M Anderson, B Meyer and P Olivier (eds), *Diagrammatic Representation and Reasoning*, Sage (Thousand Oaks, CA), 2nd edition, 2002, pp 47–64.

54   M Anderson, B Meyer and P Olivier (eds), *Diagrammatic Representation and Reasoning*.

55   Though Eyal Wiezman's work on mapping and diagramming Israeli spatial oppression activities in Gaza, and Architecture and Justice's various mapping and diagramming projects, are important on-going projects in this field.

56   See also Z Kulpa, 'Self-consistency, imprecision, and impossible cases in diagrammatic representations', *MGV*, vol 12 no 1, 2003, pp 147–160.

57   One exception is the essay on the nihilistic diagram by P Aurelli and G Mastrigli: 'Architecture After the Diagram', *Lotus International: Diagrams* (Milan), no 127, June 2006, pp 96–105.

58   M Monmonier, *How to Lie with Maps*, University of Chicago Press (Chicago), 2nd edition, 1996.

59   See, for example, the chapter 'Up, Across and Along', in T Ingold, *Lines: A Brief History*, Routledge (Oxford), 2007, pp 72–103.

Part I: Diagrams

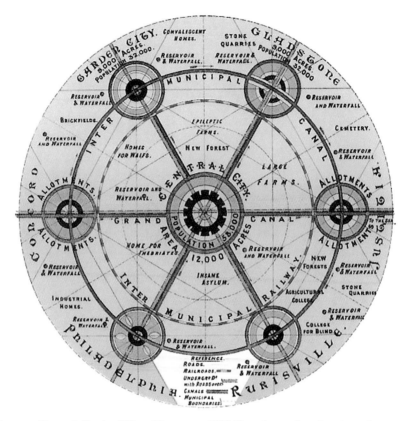

Ebenezer Howard, *Garden Cities of Tomorrow*, 1902. Plan of a garden city schematic diagram showing functional and structural divisions of a garden city and its context. Note the special zones provided for 'waifs', 'inebriates' and 'epileptics'.

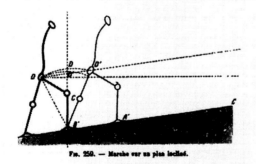

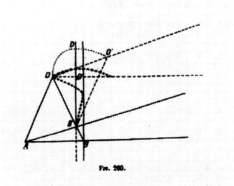

476   LE MOTEUR HUMAIN

278. En s'élevant sur un *plan incliné* (voir § 52), on se trouve dans les conditions mixtes de la marche sur escalier

Fig. 259. — Marche sur un plan incliné.

Fig. 260.

et sur terrain plat. La jambe antérieure B (*fig.* 259) est nécessairement fléchie, de sorte que OCB' = OB ; en outre, le

corps se porte en avant pour résister à la composante tangentielle de la pesanteur.

En devenant verticale, la jambe antérieure élève le poids

Movement figure from Jules Amar's *Le moteur humain*, 1914, (trans The Human Motor, 1920).

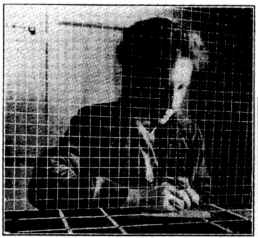

FIG. 13

Lamp attached to the hand and the cyclegraph record of its movement path, from Frank and Lillian Gilbreth, *Applied Motion Study*, 1917.

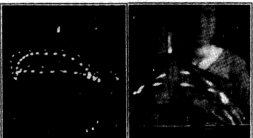

FIG. 14   FIG. 15

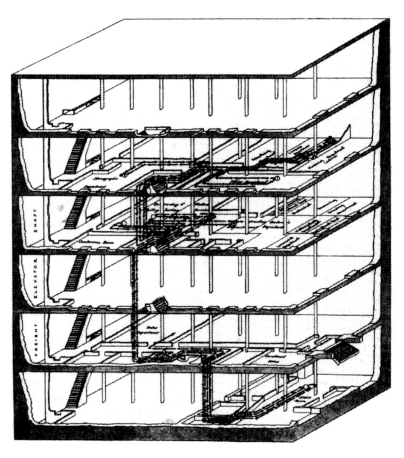

Routing diagram of proper work flow in an office, from William Leffingwell, *Office Management*, 1925.

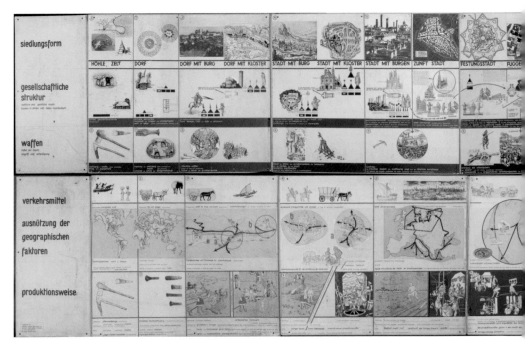

The monumental Steiger panels (1935), 16½ to 19½ feet (5–6 metres) long and about 3 feet (1 metre) or so high, are one of the grandest diagrammatic narratives of architecture and urbanism ever produced. Prefiguring the grand diagrammatic narratives of Koolhaas in his EU projects and his books on shopping and China, this large exhibition installation format diagram includes many individual diagram types. Influenced by CIAM IV and influential on Le Corbusier's CIAM Grid, it was designed in consultation with van Eesteren, Hess and Neurath and served to visualise the influence of economic and production-technical factors on the design and planning of the city considered as a social and political whole. This diagram masterpiece is radical in its encyclopaedic integration of many types of diagram. It links, for the first time in the history of architecture, critical relationships between labour, technology, architecture, product design, the working classes, and the local and global with an unprecedented range of historical, geographic and diagrammatic methods. See below for translations of the captions. © Netherlands Architecture Institute.

Festungsstadt: fortress/fortified city
Fuggerei: the first social housing area in the 16th century
Residenzstadt: residential/housing city
Landeshauptstadt: capital city
Stadtteile: district or quarter
Verkehr: traffic
Industriequartier: industrial quarter
Handelsmetropole: commercial/trading city/metropolis
wohnen: to live
Gesellschaftliche struktur: corporate or social structure
Waffen: weapons/arms and defence
(*mittel der macht angriff und verteidigung:* means of power, aggression/attack and defence)
verkehrsmittel: means of transportation
ausnutzung der geographischen faktoren: usage of the geographic factors
produktionsweise: means of production or manufacturing/methods of production/manufacturing
hohle zelt: hollow or concave tent (for whatever reason)
Dorf: village
dorf mit burg: village with castle
burg = castle
berg = mountain
dorf mit kloster: monastery village/ village with monastery
stadt mit burgen: city with castles
zunft stadt: guild/craft city

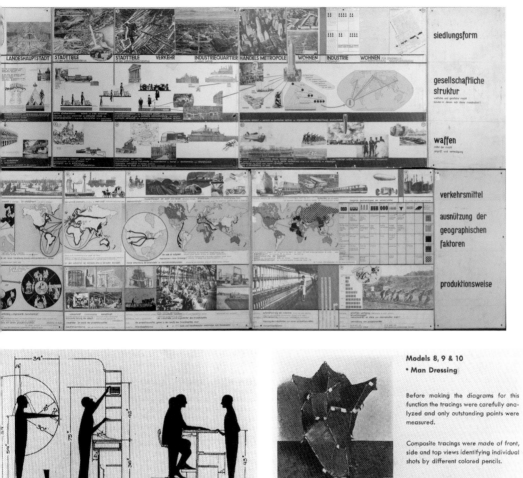

above left: Ernest Irving Freese, plate from 'Geometry of the Human Figure', *American Architect*, July 1934. Freese called these figures 'Diagrams'.

above right: 'Space shapes' of man dressing, from Jane Callaghan and Catherine Palmer, *Measuring Space and Motion*, 1943.

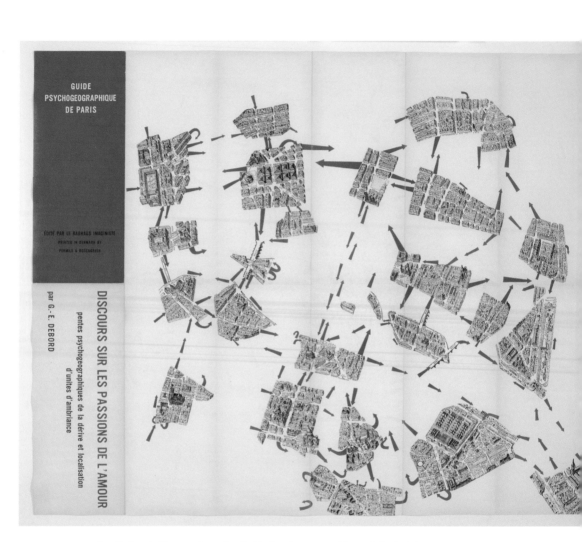

Guy Debord, diagram from the *Guide Psychogeographique de Paris: Discours sur les passions de l'amour*, 1957. © Collection FRAC Centre, Orléans. Photo Philippe Magnon. From the book published by Editions Le Bauhaus Imaginiste. Copenhagen, Permild & Rosengreen. Pentes psychogéographiques de la derive et localisation d'unités d'ambiance. Dessin. Dépliant. 59.5 x 73.5 cm (23³/₈ x 28⁷/₈ in).

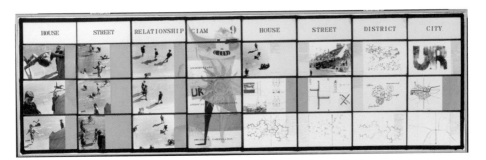

Smithsons, grid for the CIAM d'Aix in Provence 1952–3. Collage, photographs, ink on paper, glued paper. AM 1993-1-688. Introduced by Le Corbusier in 1947, the CIAM grid included nine categories of analysis: the columns' detailed milieu, use/programme, envelope volume, equipment/technology, ethics and aesthetics, socioeconomic factors, laws and regulations, finances and construction phasing. The rows of this grid by the Smithsons correlated with the main CIAM themes of living, work, development of mind and body and circulation/movement. The grid was a formal research method that explored what the Smithsons referred to as 'active socio-plastics'. © Smithson Family Collection, Paris, Musée national d'art moderne – Centre Georges Pompidou. Photo © CNAC/MNAM, Dist. RMN/© Georges Meguerditchian.

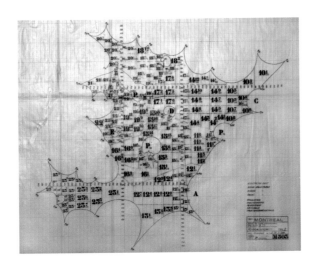

Frei Otto, numbered diagram for the cutting pattern of the membrane for the tensile German Pavilion at the Montreal Universal Expo 1965–7. © ILEK Universität Stuttgart, Germany.

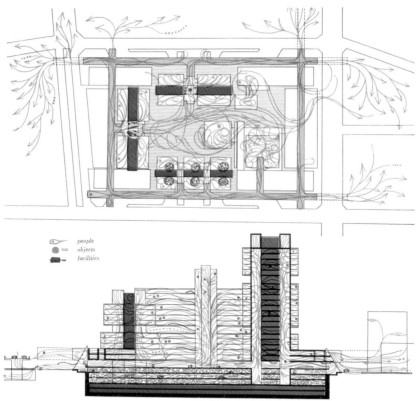

Fumihiko Maki, Dojima Development Project, Tokyo Bay, 1964. Circulation diagrams showing the relationship of people, objects and facilities. Reproduced by permission of Maki and Associates. © Fumihiko Maki.

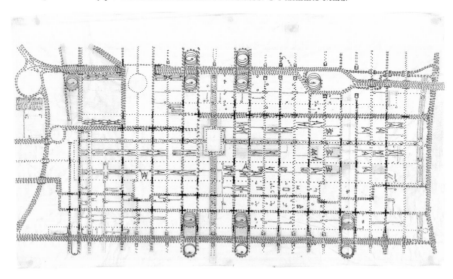

Louis Kahn, Traffic Study, project, Philadelphia, Pennsylvania, 1952. Plan of proposed traffic-movement pattern. Ink, graphite, and cut-and-pasted papers on paper, 62.2 x 108.6 cm (24¹/₂ x 42³/₄ in), Museum of Modern Art (MoMA), New York. © 2008. Digital image, The Museum of Modern Art, New York/Scala, Florence.

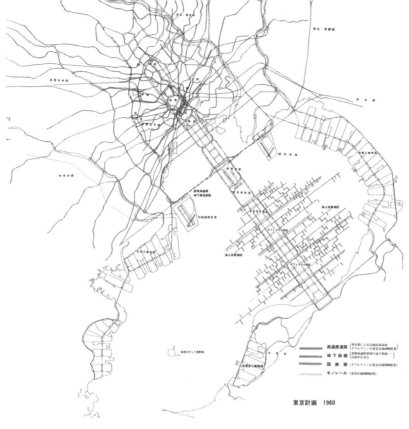

東京計画 1960

Kenzo Tange, Tange Associates, A Plan for Tokyo, 1960. The first Metabolist urban masterplan, Tange's design for an infinitely extendable, multipliable and expandable series of megastructures for Tokyo necessitated a diagrammatic approach that manages a systemic equilibrium between variability and organisation. Influenced by diagrams from technical, biological and computer systems diagrams and theories, this work went on to influence later diagram architects like MVRDV. Reproduced by permission of Tange Office © Takako Tange.

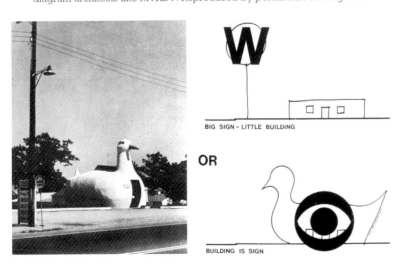

Robert Venturi, 'The Long Island Duckling'. This duck-shaped farm stand was the subject of Venturi's illustration for his thesis about a building being dominated by its symbolic form, which he contrasts with the 'decorated shed'. © Courtesy Venturi, Scott Brown and Associates.

Diagrams of Diagrams
Architectural Abstraction and Modern Representation

Anthony Vidler

In this extensive survey, Professor Antony Vidler (Dean of the Cooper Union School of Architecture, New York) analyses the history of the 20th-century architectural diagram and its role in the modern representation of architecture. His analysis explores the diagram's seeming ubiquity across almost all 'approaches and styles' of contemporary architecture. In a historical analysis from Victor Hugo in the 19th century up to the present, Vidler charts the shifting fortunes of abstraction, reduction and geometrical simplicity, some of the key qualities of the architectural diagram. Focusing on these categories, properties and effects of the diagram, he details some of the critiques raised against these modernising tendencies and qualities, including the charges that these were sterile, inhuman, degrading and alienating. Vidler describes how these same critiques are still being used against today's diagram architectures. Conversely, he shows how the same arguments about newness, purity, universality, essentialism and objectivity from diagrammatic architects today was present in the rhetoric of architects from previous centuries. Vidler's account argues that architects have, in successive historical waves, positioned themselves at various points in the history of architectural avant-gardes by privileging abstraction, reduction, purity and simplicity of geometry. Using various examples from neoclassicism to Modernism, he shows how each successive wave towards a universalising, essentialising and objectivising of architecture led to an ever-increasing and diagrammatic terseness, succinctness and economy of design, ultimately resulting in the dematerialising transparency of design and building in Modernist and contemporary architecture. One of the very few texts to significantly theorise the diagram in architecture before and in the 19th century, Vidler's lineage of the diagram also moves through Ledoux, Durand, Le Corbusier and Wittkower, to include Rowe, Koolhaas, Lynn, MVRDV and Eisenman.

… Neither a map nor a model of an existing geography, this environment is a virtual model of data as if it were geography, inserted into the morphologically transformed structures of cities and regions. Its architects refer to topologies and topographies and prefer to identify what they do as mapping rather than drawing[1] … they track movement and event in space like choreographers. Their projects and buildings share an ironic sensibility that prefers the arbitrary rigour of an imposed and consciously subverted system to any emotive expressionism. Their drawings are cool and hardline, black-and-white diagrams of functional forms[2] ... Their drawings are thin traceries of wire-frame construction, digital or not, that affirm process rather than product and refer to various traditions of the avant-garde, whether Constructivist, Dadaist, or Surrealist ... Such imaginary objects, composite portraits of contemporary architectural projects, exemplify only a few of the design tendencies that have superseded what in the last decades of the 20th century was called Postmodernism. In place of a nostalgic return to historical precedents, often couched in 'Renaissance humanist' rhetoric, these new 'blobs', 'topographies' and 'late modernisms' find their polemical stance in a resolutely forward-looking approach and their modes of design and representation in digital technologies. Radically different in their forms and aims, they nevertheless find common cause in their espousal of the one representational technique that they share with their Modernist avant-garde antecedents: their affection for what they and their critics call the 'diagram' ... This tendency is exhibited on every level of meaning associated with the term diagrammatic, and runs the gamut of a wide range of approaches and styles that at first glance seem entirely disparate – from diagrammatic caricature to theoretical discourse, Modernist revival to digital experiment ... Supporting this revival of diagrams, an entire theoretical discourse has been developed around the genre, following the coining of the term diagram architecture by the Japanese architect Toyo Ito in 1996 to characterise what he saw as a new sensibility in the work of his compatriot Kajuyo Sejima[3] ... In this ascription, architecture itself becomes joined to its diagram – a diagram of spatial function transformed transparently into built spatial function with hardly a hiccup ... Sejima herself has developed the genre into a design method of distinct clarity, where simple black-and-white diagrams of function and space are translated elegantly into building in a minimal aesthetic that goes well beyond the merely functional, in a way that has led some critics to see echoes of Japanese mysticism in the intensity of her material abstractions.[4]

From a less transcendental, and more neo-Structuralist position, Peter Eisenman, whose elegant linear projections of complicated cubic constructions, generated from a combination of historical analysis of Modernism and a study of syntactical visual language that derived from his reading of structural linguistics, became the paradigm of what the 1970s termed 'paper architecture', now finds a new intellectual receptivity for his diagrammatic drawings. His recently published *Diagram Diaries* at once reframes his life's work under a term whose revived legitimacy offers a means of inventing a pedigree for his digital experiments in morphological projection.[5] These projects and many more continue the late-modern critical and ironic investigation of the Modernist legacy of the last 20 years, while using the diagram as a device to both recall and supersede its formal canons ... The diagrammatic turn in architecture, on another level, has been quickly assimilated into design practices that work with digital techniques of representation ... Despite the resistance of many architects, who mourn the passing of the oft-claimed relations between eye and hand, the evident speed with which digitised images of traditional modes of representation (perspective axonometric, plan and so on) can be modified and worked with has for many years supported the introduction of so-called computer-aided design into practice.[6] But more significant still, what has clearly emerged in recent buildings and projects is an architecture itself not simply aided, but generated, by digital means, whether through animation, morphing or three-dimensional scanning and milling, in a way that would have been formally and technologically impossible hitherto … In projects like these, the translation of geometry into building is the more direct as a result of the intimate relations between digital representation and industrial production, so that, for example, all traditional ideas of standardisation can be jettisoned by a cutting or milling factory that runs automatically from the designer's program, as was the case with the titanium panels, all of different dimensions, that surface the vaults of Bilbao. The digital effect of these schemes is further reinforced by the use of materials with smooth reflective or translucent surfaces and of complex structures before only imagined in Expressionist or Constructivist utopias.[7]

II

Architectural drawing has always been, as Walter Benjamin remarked, a 'marginal case' with respect to the major arts.[8] In the sense that it precedes the building, that it is produced without reference to an already constituted object in the world, it has never conformed to traditional formulations of 'imitation'. In the sense that it is a drawing towards the work of art itself, it is inevitably regarded as a supplement, part of the evolutionary narrative of a building's production, but not to be valued as art per se. As the late Robin Evans noted, this is 'the peculiar disadvantage under which architects labour; never working directly with the object of their thought, always working at it through some intervening medium, almost always the drawing, while painters and sculptors, who might spend some time working on preliminary sketches and maquettes, all ended up working on the thing itself'.[9] Yet it is true, as Evans also pointed out, that the architect's drawing, as opposed to the painter's and the sculptor's, is generally the only work actually touched by the architect's hand.[10] This paradoxical separation between the artist and the work, the foundation of much architectural theory concerned with representation, was the occasion for Benjamin's remark that architectural drawings could not be said to 're-produce architecture'. Rather, he observed, 'They produce it in the first place' ('Study of Art', p 89).

Architectural drawing is also seriously 'technical' in nature, representing its objects with geometrical projections, plans and sections that demand a certain expertise of the viewer, one trained to imagine the characteristics and qualities of the spaces represented by these enigmatic lines, as well as interpret them in their context of a long tradition of spatial culture, cued to their often sly and concealed references to former architectural precedents … The architect works in code, code that is readily understood by others in the trade, but is as potentially hermetic to the outsider as a musical score or a mathematical formula. These encodings of representation have, throughout the modern period, suffered from a second level of difficulty. At a time when architecture was tied to the classical conventions, or later to the historical styles, the amateur might easily enough recognise the period or genre, identify the cultural reference and comprehend the implied commentary. Modern architectural drawings however, depict a more or less abstract object, assembled out of geometrical forms, with few recognisable building elements such as columns or decorative motifs. Abstractions of abstractions, they have increasingly over the last two centuries become little more than ciphers understood only by the professional circle around the architect, meaningless to client and layperson alike. Le Corbusier's schematic evocations of infinite space, his evocation of a building's principal elements in a few quick lines; Mies van der Rohe's perspectives, often signalled by the thinnest of pencil lines situating a plane hovering in universal, gridded, space; such drawings suspended somewhere between a design process and a diagram carry little weight as popular representations.

This apparent identity of the Modernist drawing and its object, both informed by a geometrical linearity that tends toward the diagrammatic, has, throughout the modern period, led to charges that the one is the result of the other, that architecture has too slavishly followed the conventions of its own representation. Modern architecture, concerned to represent space and form abstractly, avoiding the decorative and constructional codes of historical architectures, is thus accused of reductivism, of geometrical sterility, and thence of alienation from the human. This has been true since Victor Hugo first launched the attack in the first era of architecture's mechanisation, and the issue has periodically resurfaced over the last century to be reframed most succinctly in Henri Lefebvre's critique of Modernism's 'abstract space'[11] … In both cases, the complaint had as much to do with architecture's chosen means of representation as with the built structures themselves … Both Hugo and Lefebvre ground their indictments on what they consider the root cause of the 'fall' of architecture: representation, or more specifically, the too easy translation of the new graphic techniques used by the modern architect into built form. Architecture, that is, looked too much like the geometry with which it was designed and depicted. Geometry is thus seen as the underlying cause of architectural alienation, the degradation of humanism and the split between architecture and its 'public'. And if for Hugo architecture had become no more than the caricature of geometry, for Lefebvre architectural blueprints, and more generally the architect's fetishisation of graphic representations as the 'real', sterilised and degraded lived space. For Lefebvre, the discourse of the graphic image 'too easily becomes – as in the case of Le Corbusier – a moral discourse on straight lines, on right angles and straightness in general, combining a figurative appeal to nature (water, air, sunshine) with the worst kind of abstraction (plane geometry, modules, etc).'[12]

Such criticisms have been commonplace throughout the life of Modernism. 'Diagrammatic architecture' has been a term more of abuse than praise, signifying an object without depth, cultural or physical, one subjected to the supposed tyranny of geometry and economy – the commonplace of the 'Modernist box' caricatured by Postmodernists. As early as 1934, at the height of Modernist functionalism, the art historian and friend of Le Corbusier Henri Focillon was warning that 'in considering form as the graph of an activity ... we are exposed to two dangers. The first is that of stripping it bare, of reducing it to a mere contour or diagram. . . . The second danger is that of separating the graph from the activity and of considering the latter by itself alone. Although an earthquake exists independently of the seismograph, and barometric variations exist without any relation to the indicating needle, a work of art exists only insofar as it is form'[13] ... In this context, the diagram was to be avoided, a mechanical trap.

III

Despite such criticisms, the diagram has held a privileged place in the development of modern architecture as at once responding to the aesthetics of Rationalism and the authority of Functionalism. Beginning in the late 18th century, and in tune with the geometrical predilections of the scientific Enlightenment, a few architects began to turn away from the elaborate renderings, common to the late 18th-century academy and its heir, the Ecole des Beaux-Arts. Ledoux, trained as an engraver and inspired by the plates of Denis Diderot's *Encyclopedie*, developed a geometrical style of representation that informed his built work. The architect Jean-Nicolas-Louis Durand, appointed to the newly established Ecole Polytechnique after 1795 and responding to the demands of its new director, Gaspard Monge, developed a method for representation – a code of points, lines and planes to be organised on the newly introduced graph paper – that in his terms corresponded to the stereotomy and metric standardisation of Monge and the requirements of simplicity and economy[14]... for Durand, drawing was also a way of constructing what the philosophers had attempted to invent for centuries – a kind of universal characteristic ... Durand's diagrammatic method, economic of time and resources and readily communicable to the client, the engineer and the contractor, was widely adopted in the 19th century, although it did not, as its inventor had hoped, succeed in displacing the more elaborate renderings of the Beaux-Arts. Modernists at the end of the century, however, were quick to seize on its potential for conveying abstraction and function, among them Le Corbusier, who seized on the axonometric projections of historical structures published by the engineer Auguste Choisy in 1899, reprinting them in his articles on architecture for *L'esprit nouveau* between 1920 and 1923.[15]

Inheriting this double ideal, of a graphic representation that is itself a tool for the installation of the utopia it outlines, a geometrically driven Modernism developed a special affection for the utopian diagram. Ledoux's claims for the circle and the square as the 'letters' of the architect's 'alphabet' echoed Enlightenment projects for the development of a universal language, and his Ideal City of Chaux demonstrated the use of such geometry as a pictogrammatic language of three-dimensional form ... Le Corbusier, with an architectural sensibility informed by post-Cubist developments in painting and sculpture, psychology and philosophy, found in 'abstraction' a weapon against the historical styles and a powerful support for an architecture based on form (and its qualities of mass and surface) and space (and its qualities of enclosure or infiniteness). In this sense, abstraction was registered as a primary aesthetic quality, one that allowed for the proportional systems and historical styles formerly making up the aesthetic content of the 'art' of architecture to be superseded by its own constructive and space-enclosing elements expressed in the pure geometries now coincident with the technological potential of steel and reinforced concrete. 'Architecture has nothing to do with the "styles",' wrote Le Corbusier in 1923. 'It appeals to the highest faculties by its very abstraction. Architectural abstraction is both specific and magnificent in a way that, rooted in brute fact, it spiritualises it. The brute fact is subject to the idea only through the order that is projected upon it (figure 1).'[16] The neo-Platonic echoes of this form of abstraction were clear, and Le Corbusier openly claimed continuity from earlier classicisms – from the formal and spatial order of the Greeks, the institutional and typological order of the Romans, and the proportional systems of the modern French classicists of the 16th and 17th centuries. The representational modes for this kind of abstraction were likewise derived from the linear obsessions of neoclassicists … Thus Le Corbusier's characterisation of the architectural drawing echoes all the commonplaces of 'contour' theory after Johann Joachim Winckelmann: 'A good and noble architecture is expressed on paper by a diagram [*une épure*] so denuded that an insider's vision is needed to understand it; this paper is an act of faith by the architect who knows what he is going to do.' … The diagrammatic representations of such an abstraction were in this sense close replications of a 'new world of space', as Le Corbusier called it, that was to dissolve all traditional monumentalisms, styles, institutions and habitats in the universal flux of the abstract. Transparency, infinity, ineffability, liminality and the expansive extensions of the post-Nietzschean subject demanded as few boundary conditions as possible; the thinner the line, the more invisible the wall. Succinct and economical, the architect's 'épure' reduced a project to its essentials; it described the fundamental organisation of a building tersely and in terms that seemed to correspond to the scientific tenor of the times; it was, in some sense, the essence of the project, at once a correct and analytic representation of relations and a formal analogue to the built structure itself.

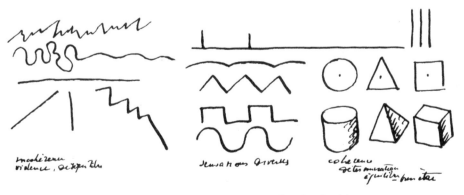

Le Corbusier, 1925. Diagram of lines and forms as they affect the physiology of sensations. © FLC/ADAGP, Paris and DACS, London 2008.

Le Corbusier's moral stance in favour of the abstract drawing had its roots in the late Enlightenment, and his attitude towards drawing was remarkably similar to that of Durand. 'Drawings', he argued late in 1939, 'are made within four walls, with docile implements; their lines impose forms which can be one of two types: the simple statement of an architectural idea ordering space and prescribing the right materials – an art form issuing from the directing brain, imagination made concrete and evolving before the delighted eyes of the architect, skilful, exact, inspired; or alternatively we can be faced with merely a dazzling spread of engravings, illuminated manuscripts or chromos, crafty stage designs to bedazzle and distract – as much their author as the onlooker – from the real issues concerned.' Architectural drawings were thus divided into two species: those that reveal the underlying structure and organisation of the project and those that dissimulate in order to seduce the lay client. This contrast between the analytical and the sentimental, the rational and the deceptive … was more than a formal distinction of representation, however; it was a touchstone by which to verify the authentic modernity of an architectural work, one that discarded the 'illusion of plans' … in favour of a design that represented its own 'idea'. The drawing – a 'simple statement of an architectural idea ordering space and prescribing the right materials' – would thereby serve as an instrument of correction and production for an architecture that, as far as possible in the translation from design to building, would represent itself transparently, so to speak, materialising its aesthetic and intellectual order as clearly as a mathematical formula.

IV

Modernist diagrams have not, however, been received without their own diagrammatic transformation at the hands of followers, epigones and revivalists. Le Corbusier's rapid sketches, diagrammatic as they were, were redolent of spatial and aesthetic potential compared with those prepared by the following generation, either in drawn or built form. Thus the polemical and geometrically closed diagrams of Albert Frey, in their attempt to clarify the principles of Modern Movement environmental ideals, rigidly codify both technology and space … Other followers of the first generation of Modernists *built* diagrammatic buildings to exemplify Modernist principles – among the best known would be Philip Johnson's quasi-Miesian Glass House in Connecticut of 1949 … and Harry Seidler's post-Marcel Breuer house for his mother, of the same year in Sydney … Such diagrams, widely repeated in the 1950s, were essential in the gradual transformation of Modernism from its status as a style for the cultural elite, or a minimal response to mass housing needs, to a generalised way of life for middle-class suburbs.

Architectural historians, as they have sought to reduce the complexity of architectural experience to formal order, have also played a role in the diagramming of space and structure, starting early enough with Paul Frankl and AE Brinckmann between 1914 and 1924.[17] Their schematic renderings of historical space prepared the way for a host of similar spatial analyses heavily informed by Gestalt psychology. Perhaps the most celebrated, and in the realm of architectural practice the most influential, was the page of systematised diagrams of Palladian villas published by Rudolf Wittkower in 1949.[18] The Wittkower diagram resonated with a post-war generation of Modernists looking for a geometrical and stable authority for form in the demonstrated absence of any single functional determinants. Alison Smithson and Peter Smithson, among others, were drawn by the idea of the existence of what might have been 'architectural principles in the age of humanism' to develop a new and rigorous geometrical Modernism.[19]

… In the same year Colin Rowe, a former pupil of Wittkower, published a seminal essay on Le Corbusier, 'The Mathematics of the Ideal Villa'[20] … Rowe's versions of the diagrams of Le Corbusier's villas at Poissy and Garches have themselves become the canonical references for late-Modernist space, referred to by architects as diverse as Rem Koolhaas, in, for example, his own mutation of the 20th-century villa in the recently completed house at Bordeaux, and Greg Lynn, in his appeal for (digital) geometry to be restored to its primary place in the generation of architecture.

The recent attention to diagrammatic form in architecture may then be seen, on one level, as a testimony to the resilience of Modernist ideologies, aesthetics and technologies among those architects who had never thoroughly embraced the return to the past championed by neohistoricists and new urbanists. Thus, continuing Modernists celebrate the diagram, in what one can only call a neo-Modernist return by many architects to Rationalist simplicity and Minimalist lucidity. Here the appeal to the diagram is both polemical and strategic. In its reduced and minimal form it dries out, so to speak, the representational excesses of Postmodernism, the citational hysteria of nostalgia and the vain attempts to cover over the inevitable effects of modern technologies, effects that Modernists had attempted to face with the invention of abstract aesthetics. In its assertion of geometry as the basis for architecture, it opens the way for a thorough digitalisation of the field … More fundamentally, the intersection of diagram and materiality impelled by digitalisation upsets the semiotic distinctions drawn by Charles Sanders Peirce as the diagram becomes less and less an icon and more and more a blueprint – or, alternatively, the icon increasingly takes on the characteristics of an object in the world.

The clearest example of this shift would be the generation of digital topographies that include in their modelling 'data' that would normally be separately diagrammed – the flows of traffic, changes in climate, orientation, existing settlement, demographic trends and the like. Formerly these would be considered by the designer as 'influences' to be taken into account while preparing a 'solution' to the varied problems they posed. Now, however, they can be mapped synthetically as direct topographical information, weighted according to their hierarchical importance, literally transforming the shape of the ground. The resulting 'map', however hybrid in conception, is now less an icon to be read as standing in for a real territory than a plan for the reconstitution of its topographical form.

… In this context, the question of architectural abstraction, whether in representation or in building, takes on an entirely new significance. For what seems to be at stake is the instability provoked between the new formal vocabularies generated by the computer and their easy translation into built form, so as to produce, almost simultaneously, an image as architecture and architecture as image. That is, where traditionally in classical and Modernist works the architecture might image an idea, be imaged itself or produce an image of its own but at the same time take its place in the world as experienced and lived structure and space, now the image participates in the architecture to an unheralded degree, a condition that calls for, if not a post-digital reaction, certainly a re-evaluation of the nature and role of abstract representation in the production of (abstract) architecture. For the question raised by the new digital diagrams is whether they are in fact abstract at all, at least in the sense of the word used by Modernist aesthetics. Where Corbusian and Miesian diagrams held within them the potential of form to be realised as abstract spatial relations – abstractions of abstractions, so to speak – the digital drawing is nothing more nor less than the mapping of three- or four-dimensional relations in two, more like an engineering specification than an abstraction. The aesthetics of digitalisation, moreover, seem driven less by a polemical belief in the virtues of an abstract representation of a new world, than by the limits of software's replication of surface, colour and texture and its notorious aversion to any ambiguity: the potential openness of the sketch, of the drawn line in all its subtleties, is reduced to thin-line clarity and all-over surface pattern. It would seem, then, that a new approach to aesthetics must be forged in the face of such drawing, one that would take into account the changing definitions of the 'real', the 'image' and the 'object' as it is subjected to the infinite morphings and distortions of animation. An aesthetics of data, of mapped information, would in these terms differentiate itself from the diagrammatic functionalism of the Modern Movement as well as from the long-lived neo-Kantianism that has served Modernism's aesthetic judgements since the Enlightenment. Modernism in these terms has shifted from a diagram that is rendered as an abstraction of an abstraction to one that is a diagram of a diagram.

Notes
1   See MVRDV, *Metacity/Datatown* (Rotterdam), 1999.
2   I am referring to recent projects by Rem Koolhaas (The House at Bordeaux, 1999; the entry for the competition for the French National Library, 1989) and by Zaha Hadid.
3   Toyo Ito, 'Diagram Architecture', *El Croquis*, vol 77 no 1, 1996, pp 18–24.
4   See, for example, Pier Luigi Nicolin, 'The Tao of Sejima', *Lotus*, no 96, 1998, pp 7–9. Nicolin takes issue with Ito's interpretation of Sejima's translucent and transparent 'membranes' as a reflection of the high-speed media metropolis and proposes instead an alternative reading – that of deceleration and slowdown. This, he argues, might represent a shift from 'a sociological, or mimetic, phase, related to the world of information processing, to a scientific, philosophical or mystical phase'.
5   Peter Eisenman, *Diagram Diaries* (New York), 1999.
6   I have sketched the historical background of this technological revolution in architecture in 'Technologies of Space/Spaces of Technology', *Journal of the Society of Architectural Historians*, vol 58 no 3, September 1999, special issue: Architectural History, 1999/2000, pp 482–6.

7   A useful review of these diverse tendencies is to be found in Peter Zellner, *Hybrid Spaces: New Forms in Digital Architecture* (New York), 1999.

8   Walter Benjamin, 'Rigorous Study of Art: On the First Volume of the *Kunstwissen-schaftliche Forschungen*' trans. Thomas Y Levin, *October*, vol 47, Winter 1988, p 89. This is a translation of Walter Benjamin, 'Strenge Kunstwissenschaft. Zum ersten Bande des *Kunstwissenschaftliche Forschungen*', *Frankfurter Zeitung*, 30 July 1933, appearing under Benjamin's pseudonym Detlef Holz; republished in Walter Benjamin, *Gesammelte Schriften* (Frankfurt am Main), 1982, vol 3, pp 363–74.

9   Robin Evans, *Translations from Drawing to Building and Other Essays* (London), 1997, p 156. The original article, 'Translations from Drawing to Building', *AA Files* no 12, Summer 1986, pp 3–18, introduced a subject that was to be developed in brilliant detail in his posthumously published *Projective Cast: Architecture and Its Three Geometries* (Cambridge, MA), 1995.

10 Indeed it is significant that the only large-scale exhibition dedicated solely to the architectural drawing mounted by a major museum in recent years was the decidedly ambiguous installation of 19th-century drawings from the Ecole des Beaux-Arts at the Museum of Modern Art, New York. Here, the obvious target was Modernism itself, the 'International Style' imported by its first architectural curator, Philip Johnson, together with Henry-Russell Hitchcock in 1932. Obviously appealing to a public said to be tired of minimalism and abstraction in architecture and a profession preoccupied with 'meaning', 'signification' and the communicative power of architecture to a broader public, this show of ideal projects had, save in its last-minute presentation of Charles Garnier's Paris Opera, little to do with actual building. For a critical review of this exhibition with regard to the tradition of the Museum of Modern Art, see William Ellis (ed), 'Forum: The Beaux-Arts Exhibition', *Oppositions*, vol 8, Spring 1977, pp 160–75.

11 See Victor Hugo, 'Guerre aux demolisseurs!' (1825–32), in *Oeuvres complètes: Critique*, ed Pierre Reynaud (Paris), 1985, p 187; Henri Lefebvre, *The Production of Space*, trans Donald Nicholson-Smith (Oxford), 1991, chap 4, 'From Absolute Space to Abstract Space'.

12 Lefebvre, *Production of Space*, p 361.

13 Henri Focillon, *The Life of Forms in Art*, trans Charles Beecher Hogan and George Rubier (New York), 1992, p 33.

14 See Werner Szambien, *Jean-Nicolas-Louis Durand, 1760–1834. De l'imitation à la norme* (Paris), 1984.

15 Auguste Choisy, *Histoire d'architecture*, 2 vols (Paris), 1899; Le Corbusier republished many of his axonometrics that displayed in one projection the space and structure of the buildings represented in the journal *L'esprit nouveau* between 1920 and 1921, and again in Le Corbusier, *Vers une architecture* (Paris), 1923.

16 Le Corbusier, *Vers une architecture*, 35. My translation.

17 See Paul Frankl, *Principles of Architectural History: The Four Phases of Architectural Style, 1420–1900*, trans James F O'Gorman (Cambridge, MA), 1968; and AE Brinckmann, 'Schematic Plans of Renaissance and Baroque Spatial Groups', *Plastik und Raum. Als Grundformen Künstlerischer Gestaltung* (Munich), 1924.

18 Rudolph Wittkower, *Architectural Principles in the Age of Humanism* (London), 1949.

19 See Reyner Banham, 'The New Brutalism', *Architectural Review*, no 118, 1955, pp 355–61.

20 Colin Rowe, 'The Mathematics of the Ideal Villa, Palladio and Le Corbusier Compared', *Architectural Review*, no 101, 1947, pp 101–4.

Representations (Berkeley), No 72, Autumn 2000, excerpts and associated notes from pages 1–20. Reproduced by permission of Anthony Vidler.
© The Regents of the University of California.

Scientific Management and the Birth of the Functional Diagram

Hyungmin Pai

In these extracts from his book *The Portfolio and the Diagram: Architecture, Discourse and Modernity in America*, Professor Hyungmin Pai (University of Seoul, Korea) offers an outline history of the architectural diagram in late 19th- and early 20th-century America. Examining the visual and textual evidence for the rise of the Modernist discourse of the architectural diagram, Pai's analysis of professional architectural journals, interior design and domestic, managerial and industrial publications explores the diagrammatic link between architectural design and social, economic, technological and industrial ideologies of innovation. Contextualised in relation to Taylorism, scientific management and the rise of Modernist functionalism, Pai's interest lies in charting the effects on architectural design of the instrumental use of space planning, circulation (routing) and the technical diagrams of new building programmes, typologies and technologies. Constructed as an objective, scientific object, the diagram, and diagramming, became the method of choice in the Modernist project to redefine architectural design research and professional practice as having the technical authority and validity of an expert and specialist science. From the work of Christine Frederick to the time-motion studies and the cyclegraphic diagrams of the Gilbreths, Pai charts the diagram's role in the functionalisation of the body and its spatial integration with the movements, materials, time and space of architecture. Addressing the relationship of the diagram to the photograph, plan and *parti*, he argues that the architectural diagram was developed (beyond Bentham's Panopticon diagram) as a problematic tool for surveillance, prediction and control. This diagrammatic engineering and quantification of organisational, social and bodily labour, behaviour and production systems as machinic and, later, as biological systems is interpreted by Pai as a claim for the design of programme as the legitimate locus of expertise, authority and validation for architectural professionals and academics. Highlighting the subjectivity and the possibilities for the expressive potential, indeterminacies, continuities and discontinuities of today's discourse of the diagram (as formulated by Christopher Alexander, Ben van Berkel and Caroline Bos, Greg Lynn, Toyo Ito and Kayuzo Sejima, among others), Pai notes the criticisms, weaknesses and limitations of the diagram that accompanied its evolution into the 21st century.

In the preceding ... we examined the new promises and demands that emerged in the midst of a fundamental transition in the architectural discipline ... different appeals to style, rationality and social relevance were part of a complex history that witnessed the formation of the discourse of the diagram. As much as this discourse spread and grew along the cracks of the discipline, it was also part of a larger social, economic and technological history ... we examined Taylorism in relation to the evolution of functional planning as a concept antithetical to architectural composition, but we did not deal with what would become its central mode of representation – the diagram ... we shall look at the logic, techniques and modes of representation of the diagram: first, as it emerges within scientific management, and second, as it shifts into the realm of architectural discourse. Though the diagram was certainly not the 'invention' of scientific management, in its attempt to shift the object of the diagram from nature to society, from machine to the human body, we begin to discover the central issues of the architectural diagram ...

Scientific management, perhaps the emblematic social technology of the past century, operated on two basic modern precepts that logically attracted it to the diagram. First of all, scientific management was one of the clearest manifestations of the separation of subject and object, and the subsequent pursuit of their reunification. Based on the authority of scientific knowledge, scientific management assumed that knowledge could be severed from practice and thus could function as the means of controlling practice. In this gap between conception and execution, the diagram emerged as a necessary mechanism for the subject to control its object of knowledge. The diagram is an essentially modern mode of representation ... Its genius lies in the invention of a discursive code that organises reality in order that it may be both visible and usable. Instrumentality, rather than resemblance, is thus the essential criterion in defining a diagram. It is the emblem of the modern crisis of representation ... The second conceptual formation that links scientific management to the birth of the diagram is that of metaphor. For all its professed instrumentality, modernity has continued to be a search for truth ... Though it was exactly the positivist project to do away with all figures of speech, to speak of 'things as they are',[1] for scientific management to apply the tools of engineering towards the control of society it became necessary to construct a set of analogies with natural and mechanical systems ... In scientific management, the production process of a factory, the daily routine of a household, a secretary's office schedule, and the curriculum of a school could each be described as a set of natural patterns ... The most basic metaphor for scientific management was that of man as machine. As David Noble pointed out, the development of modern management could itself be construed as a 'shift on the part of engineers from the engineering of things to the engineering of people'[2] ... the engineering principles of materials and equipment were easily applied to human movement and social organisation. As the terms *human engineering*, *human motor* and *human machine*, so pervasive in the literature of

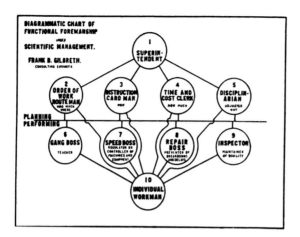

Figure 1 'Chart of Functional Foremanship under Scientific Management'.
From Frank and Lillian Gilbreth, *Applied Motion Study*, 1917.

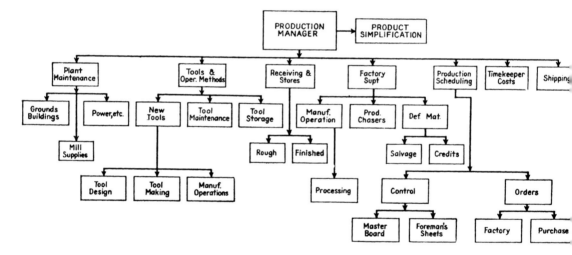

Figure 2 'Organisation Chart and Functions of Production Departments'. From
Arthur G Anderson, *Industrial Engineering and Factory Management*, 1928.

management, implied, the body of the worker was visualised and conceptualised as a
machine. This metaphor was shared with industrial psychology and the behaviourism of
John B Watson, popularised during the 1910s and 1920s. Not surprisingly, both scientific
management and behaviourism shared the goal of the 'prediction and control of human
beings'.[3] In order to actualise these cognitive and discursive constructions, a specific set
of techniques had to be developed. During the 1910s, the most meticulous techniques
of measuring and regulating the body were produced by the husband and wife team of
Frank and Lillian Gilbreth[4] ... Using Taylor's functional divisions, the Gilbreths transcribed
his system into the diagram in figure 1 In this diagram the worker was placed at the centre
of the converging lines of 'functional management', or 'functional control'.

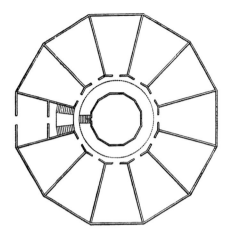

Figure 3 Diagrammatic plan of Jeremy Bentham's Panopticon, devised 1787. From John Bowring (ed), *The Works of Jeremy Bentham*, vol 4, 1843.

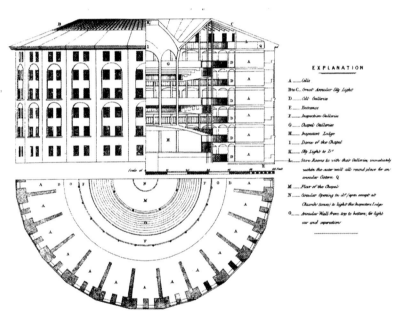

Figure 4 Example of Panopticon building proposed by Bentham. From John Bowring (ed), *The Works of Jeremy Bentham*, vol 4, 1843.

The Gilbreth diagram in figure 1 was of course an abstract model. In charting the functional relations of the various production units of a factory, this basic diagram had to be expanded and dispersed into a more multiple organisation such as that in figure 2. Following the basic principle of the Gilbreth diagram, each box in figure 2 symbolised a functional unit rather than a spatial boundary. Furthermore, these diagrams were static models; they did not address the movement of bodies, material and equipment in the factory. Subsequently implementing the Gilbreth diagram into a concrete spatial, temporal and dynamic organisation required a set of institutional mechanisms that maintained its lines of control ... In addition, according to the science of routing, the factory had to be regulated as a predictable and repetitive set of patterns ...

This was, however, an inherently paradoxical rule. In realising the diagram, space, time and movement were not only the obstacles to surveillance but also the means of maintaining functional control. It was a problem not unlike what Jeremy Bentham's Panopticon of the late 18th century was devised to solve.[5] The Panopticon, as it was drawn out in figure 3, was also a diagram. But unlike figure 1, it was a diagram of space … the Panopticon diagram is *function represented as form* … as a diagram that was meant to be built, we may construe the Panopticon as a completely functionalised space, one without dark corners of unobserved movements … However, for this building to be a spatial transcription of the Gilbreths' functional diagram, for function and space to coalesce, all the mechanisms of light and darkness, of regulating time and movement, must be perfectly implemented. Only in this panoptic utopia, only when the functionalisation and standardisation of the body are absolute, can there be such a thing as a spatial function … Though the Panopticon diagram is a spatial marking, it is a utopia, a non-place … It is in the pursuit of this utopia, this idea in architecture, that the discourse of the diagram was born. From the layout of the plant to the control of the individual worker, its operational principle was to functionalise space and spatialise function. More specifically, the diagram was used as a tool to correlate the unit of production – the functionalised body of the worker – with a spatial area … Furthermore, at the scale of each production unit, the body of the individual worker had to be integrated with its immediate material and spatial environment; thus, systematic research into the ergonomic design of tools, equipment and furniture was begun … Under these prerogatives, 'fitness' in design meant the elimination of unnecessary space and material surrounding the body … In what became widely known as their time-motion studies, the Gilbreths took long-exposure single-frame photographs of the movement of a single light point attached to the body … The principle of cyclegraphic representation could also be extended to the routing diagram … the inscription of the movements of the body-instrument produced a set of diagrams to be analysed by the management engineer, whereupon the most efficient movement pattern would be prescribed[6] …

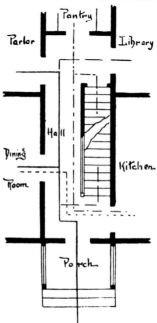

Figure 5 'The Thoroughfare'.
From Charles F Osbourne,
*Notes on the Art of House
Planning*, 1888.

Throughout the development of scientific management, graphic and linear presentation was considered the privileged form of knowledge … scientific management went one step further to become 'graphic management'. To represent a set of verbal propositions and numbers into a graph, chart or diagram was to have abstracted from empirical data a set of basic paths of control: 'Let lines replace figures' was the axiomatic principle of scientific management.[7] Though control of the human body was the ultimate purpose of these diagrams, such control required the regulation of the wayward nature of space, time and movement … As this body of ideas, techniques and markings moved on to architectural discourse, we shall see whether the functional, visual and institutional rules of scientific management could be maintained, or, if not, how they were transformed.

From Scientific Management to Architecture:
The Discursive Formation of the Architectural Diagram
 … [W]ell before the influence of scientific management, functional diagrams were a common part of 19th-century advice books and manuals on hygiene and domestic matters. The circulation diagram in figure 5, for example, appeared in an advice book titled *Notes on the Art of House Planning*, published in 1888.[8] However, … this kind of advice book was marginal to the formation of the architectural discipline. Even Christine Frederick's *The New Housekeeping*, which was immensely popular throughout American society, had little immediate impact on architecture. Though her ideas were not particularly original … Frederick's illustrations became the most widely recognised examples of the routing diagram.

The significance of Frederick's circulation diagram for architecture was more quickly grasped in Europe, particularly by German architects such as Bruno Taut and Alexander Klein. In the politically charged climate of the Weimar Republic, Frederick's book was translated and enthusiastically endorsed by both the women's movement and the Modernists in Berlin and Frankfurt.[9] During the late 1920s, Klein had developed an extensive system of architectural diagrams in his studies for the Reichsforschungsgesellschaft; these studies first introduced the routing diagram to the American journals[10] …

It was, then, in the 1930s that the new Functionalist diagram emerged as a systematic part of architectural discourse … While some diagrams can be traced directly to their roots in scientific management, for most others, particularly after the mid-1930s when the diagram became a general part of architectural discourse, it is difficult to designate a specific genealogy …

This transformation is immediately noticeable in the breakdown of the representational basis of scientific management's diagram … Not surprisingly, in Lillian Gilbreth's own contribution to kitchen planning, there were no routing diagrams … Instead, as we see in figure 6, she presented a comparison of two 'process charts' of making a coffee cake

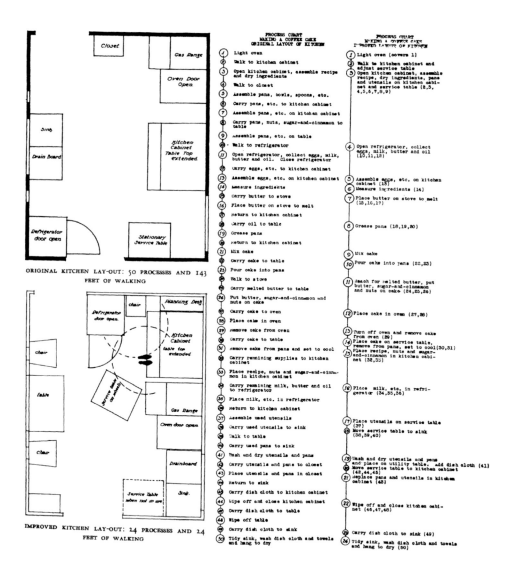

Figure 6 Lillian Gilbreth, 'Application of Motion Study to Kitchen Planning: Making a Cake'. From *Architectural Record*, March 1930.

in two different kitchen layouts. If one were to devise routing diagrams based consistently on cyclegraphic representation, even the simple task of making a cake would result in several dozen separate diagrams; or if one reduced the number of diagrams, there would be so many lines in one frame that the image would be illegible. Throughout the 1930s, the diagrams that appeared regularly in the architectural journals met with the same kind of difficulties …

We may then ask how diagrams are constructed in architectural discourse. In order to understand the logic of the architectural diagram, we must first look carefully into the changing discourse of scientific management, as its object moves from the factory to the less regimented environment of the home. One of the most interesting applications of scientific management outside of the factory can be examined in Mary Pattison's *Principles of Domestic Engineering* (1915) … For Pattison, the task of planning the house was a matter of separating and reintegrating the units rooted in the basic needs of its occupants. The plan of the home could therefore be construed as a physiological map of the human body, and routing as the pursuit of a symbiotic relation between human movement and its environment …

Moving on to the architectural diagram – as for example in figure 7, a 'functional chart' of a country house – we discover Pattison's idea of the 'logical subdivision by function'. As Pattison had done, this house was divided into basic 'functional groups' … Rather than units of production and movement, they are spatial and physical indications of proximity, accessibility and relative size. And as the functional chart became a codified part of architectural discourse, it began to provide more information on form and space. Architecture's functional chart was thus more a drawing about space and distance than about function and movement, the kind of notation we have come to call the 'bubble diagram' … the architectural diagram provided the architect with the means to represent space without drawing walls, columns and vaults …

In principle, the diagram should represent concepts and objects external to the building: the movement and activity of its occupants, the flow of air, the angle of sunlight, ie the 'function' of the building. These diagrams then play a metaphorical role: the ventilation diagram views the building as a machine for breathing; the sunlight diagram views it as a machine for controlling light and shadow … Thus, metaphor, so central to the discursive formation of scientific management, also became a pervasive trope of architecture's discourse of the diagram …

At one level, the metaphor functioned as pure ideology, one in which the architectural profession identified its role in the intervention into social institutions. It enabled American architecture to respond to the demands of efficiency and business after the First World War … It facilitated the depiction of a building as a biological or mechanical system with its own components and rhythms … these narratives read like expositions of

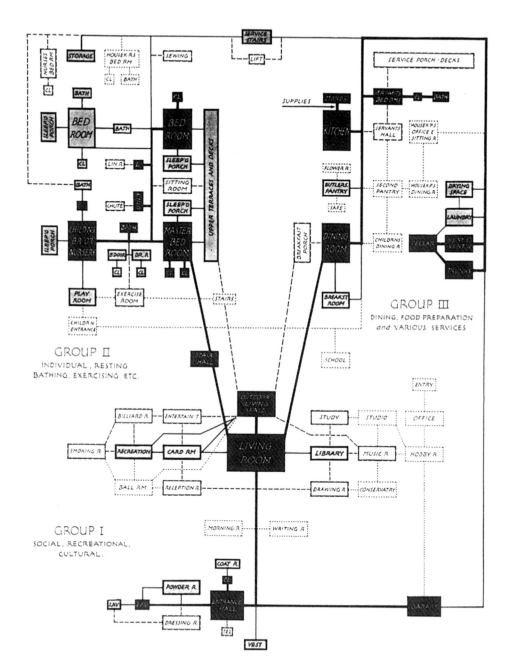

Figure 7 'The Country House Chart, Room by Room'. From *Architectural Forum*, March 1933.

While Rowe significantly notes that both positions 'condemn us to no more than simple repetition', he ultimately endorses the side of paradigm (or type) and suggests, true to his predilection for a Renaissance humanism, that it is precisely the drawing that will overcome the diagrammatic alternatives he so ably identifies but too quickly dismisses …

… The architects of the neo-avant-garde are drawn to the diagram because – unlike drawing or text, *partis pris* or bubble notation – it appears in the first instance to operate precisely between form and word. For the purposes of this brief introduction, this attitude toward the diagram has several implications: that it is fundamentally a *disciplinary* device in that it situates itself on and undoes specific institutional and discursive oppositions (and that it provides a projective discipline for new work); that it suggests an alternative mode of repetition (one which deviates from the work of the Modernist avant-gardes and envisions repetition as the production of difference rather than identity); and that it is a performative rather than a representational device (ie it is a tool of the virtual rather than the real) …

… A particular kind of repetition is at the heart of modernity, however – that of the misreading of the avant-garde – and it is this form of practice that relies on the diagram in the fullest sense …

… Advancing the potential of registering site forces and movement via inflections in generic form, Eisenman's transformational diagramming techniques anticipate the need for (and predict the possibilities of) the later development of 3-D modelling and animation software …

… Not only was the history of form rewritten, but Eisenman would subject 'form' itself to perpetual revision through an exhaustive sequence of operations: transformation, decomposition, grafting, scaling, rotation, inversion, superposition, shifting, folding, etc. And it is the catalogue of these procedures that becomes the subject matter of architecture, a disciplinary precondition to a diagrammatic approach …

Through his axonometric diagrams, Eisenman argues that Terragni develops a conceptual ambiguity by superimposing two conceptions of space – additive/layered and subtractive/volumetric – neither of which is dominant, but each of which oscillates with the other indefinitely …

… It is from this point that it might be possible to begin an evaluation of the fold in Eisenman's most recent work, for the fold is precisely a map of the event, a geometric description of the unexpected, *a diagram of the virtual*.

… The fold is perhaps the most advanced and economical device for collapsing vertical and horizontal, reversing inside and out …

... Despite the posturing by several critics and architects alike, Koolhaas and Eisenman, for example, have much more in common with each other than either the former has with Jon Jerde or the latter has with Frank Gehry. Working diagrammatically – not to be confused with simply working with diagrams – implies a particular orientation, one which displays at once both a social and a disciplinary project. And it enacts this possibility not by representing a particular condition, but by subverting dominant oppositions and hierarchies currently constitutive of the discourse ...

... Diagrammatic work is projective in that it opens new (or, more accurately, 'virtual') territories for practice, in much the way that Deleuze describes the diagrammatic painting of Francis Bacon as overcoming the optical bias of abstract art as well as the manual gesturality of action painting:

> A Sahara, a rhinoceros skin, this is the diagram suddenly stretched out. It is like a *catastrophe* happening unexpectedly to the canvas, inside figurative or probabilistic data. It is like the emergence of another world ... The diagram is the possibility of fact – it is not the fact itself.[1]

This 'emergence of another world' is precisely what the diagram diagrams ... This diagrammatic alternative can be seen initially in Eisenman's process automism and, more recently, in Koolhaas's statistical research: complementary attempts to supplant design with the diagram, to deliver form without beauty and function without efficiency.

A diagrammatic practice (flowing around obstacles yet resisting nothing) – as opposed to the tectonic vision of architecture as the legible sign of construction (which is intended to resist its potential status as either commodity or cultural speculation) – multiplies signifying processes (technological as well as linguistic) within a plenum of matter, recognising signs as complicit in the construction of specific social machines. The role of the architect in this model is dissipated, as he or she becomes an organiser and channeller of information, since rather than being limited to the decidedly vertical – the control and resistance of gravity, a calculation of statics and load – 'forces' emerge as horizontal and non-specific (economic, political, cultural, local and global). And it is by means of the diagram that these new matters and activities – along with their diverse ecologies and multiplicities – can be made visible and related. Against some of the more currently naive extensions to the legacies of Eisenman and Koolhaas, it is thus important to avoid confining a diagrammatic approach to architecture as the expression of either presumed biomathematical imperatives or socioeconomic inevitabilities, and understand architecture rather as a discursive-material field of cultural-political plasticity. To do otherwise would be to return to the inadequately diagrammatic options first outlined by Rowe (in terms of formal or analytical 'truth') and Alexander (operational or synthetic 'truth') ...

Note

1 Gilles Deleuze, 'The Diagram', in Constantin V Boundas (ed), *The Deleuze Reader*, Columbia University Press (New York), 1993, pp 194, 199.

Theories and Manifestoes, C Jencks and Karl Kropf (eds), Wiley–Academy, a division of John Wiley & Sons Ltd (Chichester), 2008. Originally published in Peter Eisenman (Introduction by Robert E Somol), *Diagram Diaries*, Universe Publications (New York), 1999. Excerpts from pp 7, 16, 21, 23–4. © Reprinted courtesy of Universe Publishing, a division of Rizzoli International Publications Inc, and Robert E Somol, 1999.

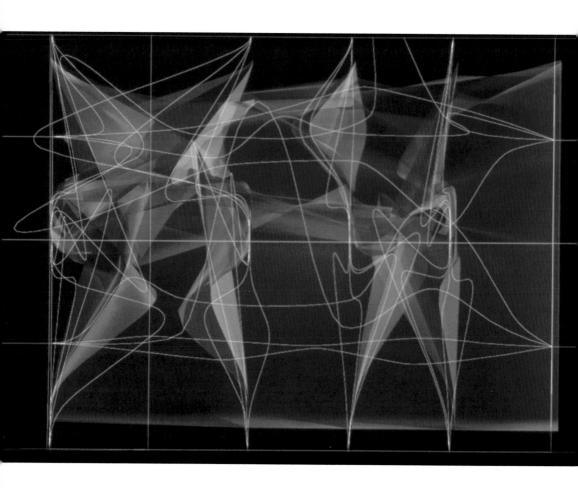

Eisenman Architects, Virtual Plan, Virtual House, Berlin, Germany, 1997.

Reproduced by permission of Eisenman Architects. © Eisenman Architects.

Diagram
An Original Scene of Writing

Peter Eisenman

Architect and theorist Professor Peter Eisenman (Cooper Union, Yale University and Principal, Eisenman Architects, New York), has generated perhaps the single most important research project on the diagram in architecture. From his PhD thesis and other texts to designs and built projects, Eisenman's work has consistently been determined by and depended on his rigorous and decades-long research into the architectural diagram. A seminal text in architectural diagram theory, this essay was first published in Eisenman's *Diagram Diaries* (1999) and has since become one of the most recent, significant and original contributions to architectural theory. The central subject of this essay is architecture's and the architectural diagram's relationship to writing and the text. For Eisenman, the diagram traces and writes, and can be traced and read in, architecture. As such, the diagram mediates between the history of architecture (diagrams of anteriority) and the ways in which this is traced in a real building and the other possible buildings that are within it (diagrams of interiority). Diagrams of exteriority, those from outside architecture, are defined as agents from the 'specific site, the programme, or the history'. Through his concept of 'superposition', Eisenman's account of the diagram demonstrates a close reading of Derridean deconstruction and other Postmodern, post-Structuralist theories of the diagram, language, text and writing which are together marshalled to critique 'the premise of architecture's origin in presence'. Effectively placing architecture on a new ontological, metaphysical and epistemological basis, this account uses the diagram to expand architecture into a more complex concept. Drawing on such diverse fields as metaphysics, aesthetics, psychology and literary theory, Eisenman references Villard d'Honnecourt, Palladio, Serlio and Le Corbusier from the history of architecture as well as such diverse thinkers as Wittkower, Freud, Foucault and Deleuze. This central text in his theoretical corpus introduces many of the concepts and lines of thought that he was to elaborate in other essays in *Diagram Diaries*, and in a second, later book on the diagram, *Feints* (2005), and through designs and built projects around the world.

As in all periods of supposed change, new icons are thrust forward as beacons of illumination. So it is with the idea of the diagram. While it can be argued that the diagram is as old as architecture itself, many see its initial emergence in Rudolf Wittkower's use of the nine-square grid in the late 1940s to describe Palladian villas. The diagram's pedigree continued to develop in the form of the nine-square problem as practised in the American architectural academy of the late 1950s and early 1960s, when it was seen as an antidote to the bubble diagramming of the Bauhaus functionalism rampant at Harvard in the late 1940s and to the *parti* of the French academy that was still in vogue at several East Coast schools well into the late 1960s. As a classical architectural diagram, the *parti* was embodied with a set of pre-existent values such as symmetry, the *marche* and *poché*, which constituted the bases of its organising strategy. The bubble diagram attempted to erase all vestiges of an embodied academicism in the *parti*. In so doing, it also erased the abstract geometric content of the nine-square.

Generically, a diagram is a graphic shorthand. Though it is an ideogram, it is not necessarily an abstraction. It is a representation of something in that it is not the thing itself. In this sense, it cannot help but be embodied. It can never be free of value or meaning, even when it attempts to express relationships of formation and their processes. At the same time, a diagram is neither a structure nor an abstraction of structure. While it explains relationships in an architectural object, it is not isomorphic with it.

In architecture the diagram is historically understood in two ways: as an explanatory or analytical device and as a generative device. Although it is often argued that the diagram is a post-representational form, in instances of explanation and analysis the diagram is a form of representation. In an analytical role, the diagram represents in a different way from a sketch or a plan of a building. For example, a diagram attempts to uncover latent structures of organisation, like the nine-square, even though it is not a conventional structure itself. As a generative device in a process of design, the diagram is also a form of representation. But unlike traditional forms of representation, the diagram as a generator is a mediation between a palpable object, a real building, and what can be called architecture's interiority. Clearly this generative role is different from the diagram in other discourses, such as in the parsing of a sentence or a mathematical or scientific equation, where the diagram may reveal latent structures but does not explain how those structures generate other sentences or equations. Similarly, in an architectural context, we must ask what the difference is between a diagram and a geometric scheme. In other words, when do nine squares become a diagram and thus more than mere geometry?

Wittkower's nine-square drawings of Palladio's projects are diagrams in that they help to explain Palladio's work, but they do not show how Palladio worked. Palladio and Serlio had geometric schema in mind, sometimes explicit and sometimes implicit, which they drew into their projects. The notations of dimensions on the Palladian plans do not correspond to the actual project but to the diagram that is never drawn. A diagram implicit in the work is often never made explicit. For example, as Kurt Forster has noted, in the earliest parchment drawings in architecture, a diagrammatic schema is often drawn or etched into the surface with a stylus without being inked. The later inking of the actual project over this then becomes a superposition of a diagrammatic trace. In many of these drawings – from late Gothic architecture to the Renaissance – the overlay does not

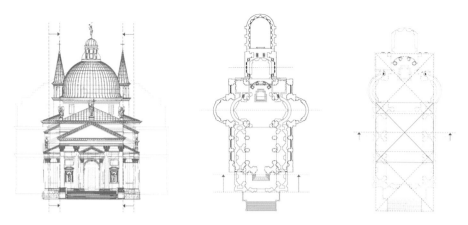

Peter Eisenman, Diagrams of Anteriority, 1982. Analytical diagrams of the Church of the Redeemer, by Andrea Palladio, Venice, Italy. Reproduced by permission of Peter Eisenman. © Peter Eisenman.

actually take all of the diagrammatic imprint, only partial traces of it. The quality of the ink on the page changes where it runs over the diagram as opposed to the places where the diagram is actually part of the plan of the building. Thus, there is a history of an architecture of traces, of invisible lines and diagrams that only become visible through various means. These lines are the trace of an intermediary condition (that is, the diagram) that exists between what can be called the anteriority and the interiority of architecture; the summation of its history as well as the projects that could exist are indexed in the traces and the actual building.

The diagram is not only an explanation, as something that comes after, but it also acts as an intermediary in the process of generation of real space and time. As a generator there is not necessarily a one-to-one correspondence between the diagram and the resultant form. There are many instances, for example in Le Corbusier's Modulor, where the diagram is invisible in the building, yet it reappears as a repetitive element that occurs at many different scales, repeated in little segments of houses to large segments of urban plans, yet it is rarely an explicit form. Thus Le Corbusier's statement that the plan is the generator will be seen to be different from the diagram is the generator. There are many examples of diagrams where a variety of shapes can be arrived at through a geometry that is exfoliated into different shapes. For example, Villard d'Honnecourt used geometric matrices to evolve natural and animal forms. One of the most interesting is the manifestation of a camel drawn from interlocking squares and diagonals. In the chateau architecture of the Loire valley in the 16th century there are irregular forms that could only have been produced through some sort of manipulation of diagrammatic geometry into a three-dimensional process called 'stereotomy'. Stones were cut from templates generated by these kinds of diagram. As Kurt Forster notes, in the late Gothic, for example, there is a diagrammatic process that leads the schematic articulation of foliage on column capitals to change from a stylised or conventional nature with bilateral symmetries to a more naturalistic, free-form nature. Such a process differs from the straightforward manipulation of geometry that was the tradition in

Gothic leaf capitals. The naturalistic evolution of these other capitals comes not from geometry but from a diagram. In this sense, the diagram becomes an intermediary condition between a regular base geometry and the capital itself. Here the diagram acts neither as geometry nor as the existent capital. It is a trace or phantom, which acts between something which can be called the interiority of architecture and the specific capital; between some explicit geometric formation which is then transformed by the diagram or intermediary process on to a result.

Reacting against an understanding of the diagram that characterised it as an apparently essentialist tool, a new generation, fuelled by new computer techniques and a desire to escape its perceived Oedipal anxieties – with regard to the generation of their mentors – is today proposing a new theory of the diagram based partly on Gilles Deleuze's interpretation of Foucault's recasting of the diagram as 'a series of machinic forces', and partly on their own cybernetic hallucinations. In their polemic, the diagram has become a keyword in the interpretation of the new. This question challenges both the traditional geometric bases of the diagram and the sedimented history of architecture, and in so doing they question any relation of the diagram to architecture's anteriority or interiority.

The second point Deleuze makes is that the diagram is different from structure. The classical architectural idea of a diagram exhibits a belief in structure as something that is hierarchical, static and has a point of origin. Deleuze says that a diagram is a supple set of relationships between forces. It forms unstable physical systems that are in a perpetual disequilibrium. Deleuze says that diagrams that deal with distribution, serialisation and formalisation are all structural mechanisms in that they lead to structure and a belief in structuring as an underlying principle of organisation. If a structure is seen as a vertical or hierarchical ordering of its constituent parts, the diagram must be conceived both horizontally and vertically, both as a structure and something which resists structuring: 'From one diagram to the next, new maps are drawn; thus there is no diagram that does not also include besides the points which it connects up (that is, besides its structural component) certain relatively free or unbound points, points of creativity, change and resistance to that existing building.' In this sense, diagrams are those forces which appear in every relation from one point to another, as superimposed maps. The distinction between Deleuze's idea of superimposition and my use of the term superposition is critical in this context. Superimposition refers to a vertical layering differentiating between ground and figure. Superposition refers to a coextensive, horizontal layering where there is no stable ground or origin, where ground and figure fluctuate between one another.

Thus diagrams for Deleuze must have a non-structuring or informal dimension. It is 'a functioning abstracted from any obstacle or friction, detached from any specific use'. This is an important movement away from the classical idea of an architectural diagram. Deleuze says that 'a diagram is no longer an auditory or visual archive, but a map, a cartography that is coextensive with the whole social field. It is an abstract machine.'

This abstract machine is defined by its functioning in unformed matter, as a series of processes that are neither mechanical nor organic. The diagram then is both form and matter, the visible and the articulable. Diagrams for Deleuze do not attempt to bridge the gap between these pairs, but rather attempt to widen it, to open the gap to other unformed matters and functions which will become formed. Diagrams, then, form visible matter and formalise articulable functions.

RE Somol follows Deleuze in situating these ideas of the diagram in architecture. For Somol, diagrams are any kind of explanatory abstraction: 'cartoons, formulas, diagrams, machines, both abstract and concrete. Sometimes they are simply found and other times they are manipulated.' A partial list of what Somol labels as 'previous' diagrams includes the nine-square, the Panopticon, the Domino, the skyscraper, the duck and the decorated shed, the fold, and bachelor machines. Somol says that he is searching for an alternative way of dealing with architecture's history, 'one not founded on resemblance and return to origins but on modes of becoming an emergence of difference'. The problem with this idea of the diagram as matter, as flows and forces, is that it is indifferent to the relationship between the diagram and architecture's interiority, and in particular to three conditions unique to architecture: (1) architecture's compliance with the metaphysics of presence; (2) the already motivated condition of the sign in architecture; and (3) the necessary relationship of architecture to a desiring subject.

Somol's argument for a diagrammatic project takes as axiomatic that every design project, whether in practice or in the university, needs to take up anew the issue of what constitutes the discipline or, in other words, that architecture both as a discipline and a social project needs to suspend and rearrange ruling oppositions and hierarchies currently in operation. This would suggest that design projects and processes cannot simply be derived from their contexts, but rather must *transform* their very social and intellectual contexts. In this sense, Somol's diagrammatic process, as a machinic environment, is already given as a social project. That is, it is not abstract or autonomous, but rather presumes that architecture already contains in its being (ie its interiority) the condition of the social.

If in the interiority of architecture there is a potentially autonomous condition that is not already socialised or that is not already historicised, one which can be distilled from a historicised and socialised interiority, then all diagrams do not necessarily take up new disciplinary and social issues. Rather, diagrams can be used to open up such an autonomy to understand its nature. If this autonomy can be defined as singular because of the relationship in architecture between sign and signified, and if singularity is also a repetition of difference, then there must be some existing condition of architecture in order for it to be repeated differently. This existing condition can be called architecture's interiority. When there is no interiority, that is, if there is no relationship between interiority and the diagram, there is no singularity which defines architecture.

If architecture's interiority can be said to exist as a singular rather than dialectical manifestation of a sign that contains its own signified, the motivation of the sign is already internalised and thus autonomous. Yet if the diagram is already social, as Somol suggests, this definition immediately historicises autonomy. The notion of the diagram being proposed here attempts to overcome the historicisation of the autonomy of architecture, that is, the already motivated nature of architecture's sign.

In this context, the relationship between the diagram and architecture's interiority is crucial. Foucault's understanding of an archive as the historical record of a culture, and of an archaeology as the scientific study of archival material, can be translated as architecture's anteriority and interiority. These cannot by their very nature be constituted merely by unformed matter, as Somol suggests, but in fact already contain presence, motivated signs and a psychical desire for delineation by the subject of both ground and figure. A diagram of instability, of matter and flows, must find a way to accommodate these concerns specific to architecture. In this context, another idea of the diagram can be proposed, one which begins from Jacques Derrida's idea of writing as an opening of pure presence.

For Derrida, writing is initially a condition of repressed memory. The repression of writing is also the repression of that which threatens presence, and since architecture is the *sine qua non* of the metaphysics of presence, anything that threatens presence would be presumed to be repressed in architecture's interiority. In this sense, architecture's anteriority and interiority can be seen as a sum of repressions. While all discourses, Derrida would argue, contain repressions that in turn contain an alternative interior representation, architecture must be seen as a special case because of its privileging of presence. If Derrida is correct, there is already given in the interiority of architecture a form of representation, perhaps as the becoming unmotivated of the architectural sign. This repressed form of representation is not only interior to architecture, but anterior to it. It is this representation in architecture that could also be called a writing. How this writing enters into the diagram becomes a critical issue for architecture.

House II, Plexiglass, 1969–70.
Reproduced by permission of Peter Eisenman. © Peter Eisenman.

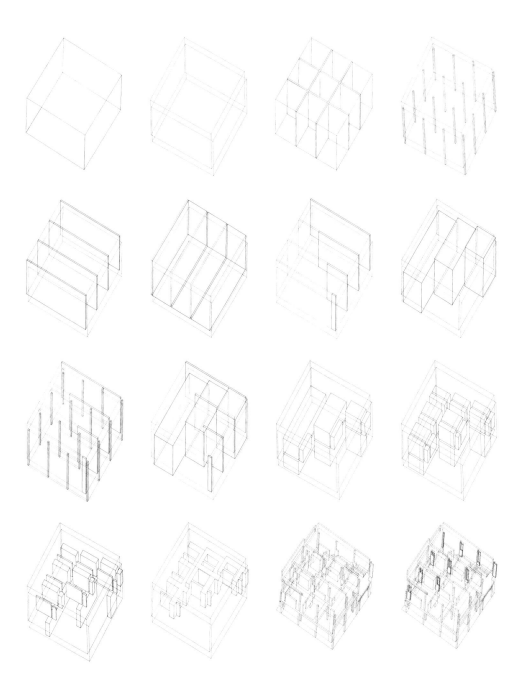

Peter Eisenman, House II, 1969–70. Diagrams of interiority: developmental sequence of the diagrams for House II showing the shifting, doubling and layering operations in the design process. Reproduced by permission of Peter Eisenman. © Peter Eisenman.

One way that memory overcomes forgetting is through mnemonic devices. Written lists are a form of mnemonic device, but one that is graphic and literal; they do not represent or contain a trace. In architecture, literal notations can produce a plan but they have nothing to do with the diagram, because a plan is a literal mnemonic device. A plan is a finite condition of writing, but the traces of writing suggest many different plans. It is the idea of the trace that is important for any concept of the diagram, because unlike a plan, traces are neither fully structural presences nor motivated signs. Rather, traces suggest potential relationships, which may both generate and emerge from previously repressed or unarticulated figures. But traces in themselves are not generative, transformative or even critical. A diagrammatic mechanism is needed that will allow for both preservation and erasure and that can simultaneously open up repression to the possibility of generating alternative architectural figures which contain these traces.

Derrida says, 'We need a single apparatus that contains a double system, a perpetually available innocence and an infinite reserve of traces.' A diagram in architecture can also be seen as a double system that operates as a writing both from the anteriority and the interiority of architecture as well as from the requirements of a specific project. The diagram acts like a surface that receives inscriptions from the memory of that which does not yet exist – that is, of the potential architectural object. This provides traces of function, enclosure, meaning and site from the specific conditions. These traces interact with traces from the interiority and the anteriority to form a superposition of traces. This superposition provides a means for looking at a specific project that is neither condemned to the literal history of the anteriority of architecture, nor limited by facts, the reality of the particular site, programme, context or meaning of the project itself. Both the specific project and its interiority can be written on to the surface of a diagram that has the infinite possibility of inscribing impermanent marks and permanent traces. Without these permanent traces there is no possibility of writing in the architectural object itself.

If architecture's interiority is seen as already written, then Derrida's use of Freud's double-sided Mystic Writing Pad could be one model for describing a conception of a diagram different from both the traditional one in classical architecture and the one proposed by Somol. Neither of these considers in any detail architecture's problem with the metaphysics of presence, the unmotivating of the sign, or the psychical problem of repression in both the interiority of architecture and in the subject. The analogy of the Mystic Writing Pad is useful because the specific conditions of site and the anteriority of architecture both constitute a form of psychical repression.

The Mystic Writing Pad, as proposed in Freud's analogy, consists of three layers: the outer layer or surface where the original writing takes place, a middle layer on which the writing is transcribed, and underneath, a tablet of impressionable material. Using a stylus, one writes on the top surface. Because of the surface underneath, the top surface reveals a series of black lines. When the top surface is lifted from the other two, the black lines disappear. What remains is the inscription on the bottom surface, the trace of the lines that have been drawn. The indentations made by the stylus remain, always present. Thus there are infinite possibilities for writing and rewriting on the top surface and a means of recording the traces of this writing as a series of superpositions on the tablet underneath. This recalls the traces of the earliest incisions on parchment that already exist in the anteriority of architecture as described above.

The architectural diagram, like the Mystic Writing Pad, can be conceived of as a series of surfaces or layers which are both constantly regenerated and at the same time capable of retaining multiple series of traces. Thus, what would be seen in an architectural object is both the first perceptual stimulus, the object itself, along with its aesthetic and iconic qualities, and another layer, the trace, a written index that would supplement this perception. Such a trace would be understood to exist before perception, in other words, before a perception is conscious of itself.

Derrida says, 'Memory or writing is the opening of that process of appearance itself. The "perceived" may only be read in the past, beneath perception and after it.' The diagram understood as a strata of superposed traces offers the possibility of opening up the visible to the articulable, to what is within the visible. In this context, architecture becomes more than that which is seen or which is present; it is no longer entirely a representation or an illustration of presence. Rather, architecture can be a re-presentation of this intervening apparatus called the diagram. In this sense, the diagram could be understood to exist before the anteriority and the interiority of architecture. It exists as the potential space of writing, a writing which supplements the idea of an interiority before perception. This idea of an interiority as containing a palimpsest of an already written undercuts the premise of architecture's origin in presence.

But there is also a temporality involved in the processes of the diagram. Derrida says that the Mystic Pad includes in its structure what Kant describes as the three modes of time: permanence, succession and simultaneity. The diagram, like the writing pad, contains the simultaneity of the appearance on its surface, what would be akin to the black lines on the top layer of the pad, as well as the indentations in the wax below: the second aspect of the time of the diagram is succession, which is akin to the lifting up of the pad and is involved in erasure and the posting of a new image. This is the permanence in the wax itself. The diagram presents in such a context a discontinuous conception of time as the periodicity and the spacing of writing. These three conditions of time are not linear or connected in a narrative way. Thus, the diagram is an intermediate or interstitial condition which lies between in space and time – between the architectural object and the interiority of architecture.

Writing implies that in an architectural object, the object's presence would already contain a repetition. In this sense an architectural object would no longer be merely a condition of being, but a condition which has within itself both a repetition of its being

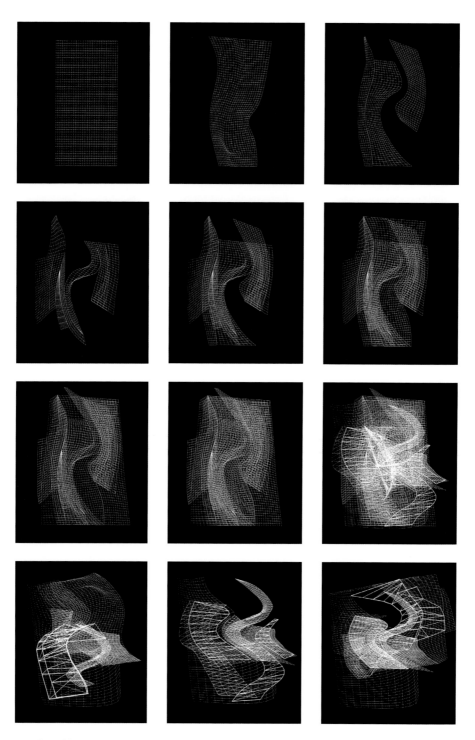

Peter Eisenman, Staten Island diagrams, Staten Island Institute. 1997–8. Diagrams of exteriority: sequence showing the superposition and laminar flows diagrams for the Staten Island Institute competition project. Reproduced by permission of Eisenman Architects. © Eisenman Architects.

and a representation of that repetition. If the interiority of architecture is singular as opposed to dialectical, and if that singularity can be defined as a repetition of difference, then architecture's interiority may be already written.

There is a second concern that the diagram must address, and that is the potential for the becoming unmotivated of the sign. The already written introduces the idea of the index into the architectural object. The index is the first movement away from a motivated sign. Here, another layer must be added to the strata of the diagram, one which, through a process of blurring, finds new possibilities for the figural within architecture's interiority that could not have come from that interiority. An external condition is required in the process, something that will introduce a generative or transformative agent as a final layer in the diagrammatic strata. This external agent is not the expression of a desiring subject, but rather must come from outside of architecture as some previously unfigured, yet immanent agent in either the specific site, the programme or the history. It could take the form of a transparent pattern or screen, which causes the already imprinted to appear as other figurations, both blurring and revealing what already exists. This is similar to the action of a moiré pattern or filter, which permits these external traces to be seen free of their former architectural contexts.

The diagram acts as an agency which focuses the relationship between an authorial subject, an architectural object and a receiving subject; it is the strata that exist between them. Derrida says that 'Freud, evoking his representation of the psychical apparatus, had the impression of being faced with a machine which would soon run by itself. But what was to run by itself was not a mechanical representation or its imitation but the psyche itself.' The diagrammatic process will never run without some psychical input from a subject. The diagram cannot 'reproduce' from within these psychical conditions. The diagram does not generate in and of itself. It opens up the repression that limits a generative and transformative capacity, a repression that is constituted in both the anteriority of architecture and in the subject. The diagram does not in itself contain a process of overcoming repression. Rather, the diagram enables an author to overcome and access the history of the discourse while simultaneously overcoming his or her own psychical resistance to such an act. Here, the diagram takes on the distancing of the subject-author. It becomes both rational and mystical, a strange superposition of the two. Yet according to Freud, only the subject is able to reconstitute the past; the diagram does not do this. He says, 'There must come a time when the analogy between this apparatus and the prototype will cease to apply. It is true that once writing has been erased the Mystic Pad cannot "reproduce" it from within; it could be a Mystic Pad indeed if, like our memory, it could accomplish that.'

Diagram Diaries, P Eisenman, Thames & Hudson (London), 1999. Originally published by Universe Publishing (New York), 1999. Excerpts pp 277–9, 281–5. Images not previously published with original text. Reproduced by permission of Peter Eisenman. © Peter Eisenman 1999.

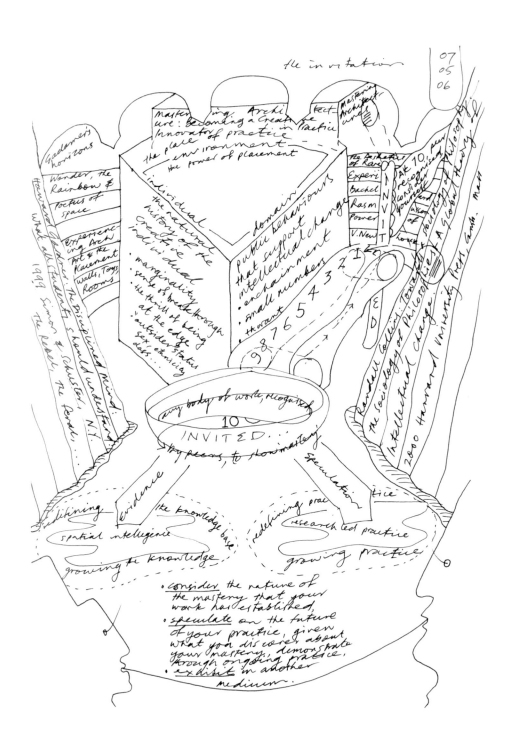

Poetics of the Ideogram

Leon van Schaik

In his new essay, Professor Leon van Schaik (School of Architecture, RMIT, Melbourne) examines the poetics of the diagram. Distinguishing between the diagram and the ideogram, van Schaik describes the context and circumstances of his personal engagement with the ideogram. He illustrates and outlines the complex genealogy of his use of the ideogram by contextualising his argument with artists as well as architects. Referencing Le Corbusier, Louis Kahn, the Smithsons, Richard Hamilton, the Situationists, Louis Aragon, Paul Klee, Sergei Eisenstein and Gordon Pask, he also withholds a special place for Saul Steinberg, whom he refers to as the 'supreme master' of the ideogram. Comparing ideograms to 'memory theatres', van Schaik argues that it is their dramaturgic distilling, encapsulation and mixing of ideas, concepts, desires and emotions that allows them to become stages for the discovery of new knowledge.

Possibly there are two histories for every phenomenon: that which the patient (but opinionated) historian uncovers through years of scholarship around a topic, and that which is the record of an individual's experience in encountering and engaging the topic. I am not a historian but I can point to a personal collection of landmarks in the making of ideograms and their poetic use, and I do have a history in making and using ideograms, which is individual to me but is inspired by exemplars that I knew surrounded me, and by histories of which I was barely aware, but of which I have become somewhat more aware.

First, why do I use 'ideogram' rather than 'diagram'? The distinction between them offered up by the Oxford English Dictionary suffices, and rescues me from the accusing gesture that fingers a 'jargon'. A diagram 'shows the features of an object needed for exposition rather than its actual appearance', while an ideogram 'symbolises the idea' of a situation. I see the ideogram as cupping a situation in your hands, embracing everything that you know and feel about it. As I comb through my library looking at architects' drawings I find many visualisations of buildings-to-be, many sketches of admired situations in the actual world, a few diagrams – fewer ideograms.

Perhaps Le Corbusier's 'The Lesson of Rome' (*Towards a New Architecture*, 1927), with a set of platonic solids hovering in the air above a bird's-eye view of a reconstructed Rome, is an ideogram, suggesting as it does the mediation between idea and its realisation,

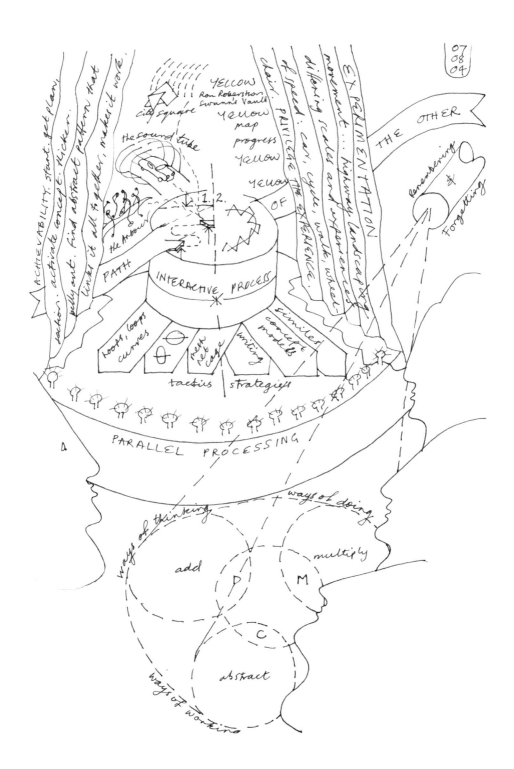

while his sketch map of Manhattan, identifiable because perforated by Central Park, surrounded by cloudy shapes roughly approximating to Queens and other adjacent suburbs each labelled 'sterile', is a diagram.[1]

None of us is innocent of these drawings, any more than we are of Louis Kahn's project for Philadelphia city centre (1956–62) which surrounded the centre with circular citadels that swallowed up the traffic entering (so many 'Pac men' chewing up, as those simulacrums of blood corpuscles do, all that is unwanted in the flows) – clearing the ground for Ed Bacon's dream of axes and plazas. Urban Design has diagrammed more than architecture and to worse effect,[2] even Peter and Alison Smithson endorsing the turning of Soho in London into something looking like an anatomical drawing of a muscle. We grew up with these diagrams. Early in my career I too made such diagrams, and some – those unpacking the basic moves in John Soane's architecture[3] – made a perhaps novel contribution to the genre.

Uneasily I watched some of my peers becoming tangled up in Piranesi, which seemed to lead them to Escher; always a solipsistic dead end, these enthusiasms for drawings as three-dimensional puzzles. Better to follow Saul Steinberg, often a supreme master of the ideogram, as in his views of the world as seen from New York looking east across an Atlantic shrunk to a stream, a plate of Europe and Asia disturbed by Alps, and then another stream for the Pacific and Los Angeles looming on the horizon; and his view from New York looking west across the Hudson River to a swathe of territory hemmed in by Canada and Mexico, punctuated with some outcrops, adjacent to one of which is Los Angeles, and looming on the horizon beyond a thin strip of the Pacific are China, Japan and Russia.[4]

Why then the ideogram? In the years after the Second World War a desire to capture 'the situation' in all of its cultural complexity and layering came into being in most fields. For me it was heralded by Richard Hamilton's *Just what is it that makes today's homes so different, so appealing?* (1956),[5] the author of which I set off in search of, and whose intent I later had confirmed by his *Hers is a lush situation* (1958) with its acknowledgement of sensuality, branding ('She' is represented by lipstick lips and one cup of a Maidenform bra) and place ('She' is in a Buick Electra in the wrap-around windscreen of which is reflected the United Nations Building in Manhattan). The connection to Wittgenstein's 'state of affairs' did not escape notice. Though I did not know it at the time, the Situationists[6] were in hot pursuit, and had even trademarked the name! Though they produced ideographic models rather than ideograms.

Leon van Schaik, ideogram of Denton Corker Marshall, prepared for the exhibition Melbourne Masters Architecture, 2004–5, TarraWarra Museum of Art, Victoria, Australia. The profiles suggest the three principals considering who might be observing them observing themselves … This engagement lead to the book *Non Fictional Narratives* (Birkhäuser, 2008) by L van Schaik. © Leon van Schaik.

When in the late 1960s at the Architectural Association I became preoccupied by my 'West London Project', much of what I needed to convey was situational, and driven by an awakened realisation that the players in an urban area all perceived of that place through their own histories in space and in culture, and that their moods influenced those perceptions, and like most of my contemporaries and near contemporaries – Bernard Tschumi,[7] Jenny Lowe,[8] Nigel Coates[9] – I was not content to leave the city to Le Corbusier's platonic solids, but felt it necessary to deal in some way with the narratives of the city. Aragon's Paris peasant and the film techniques of Eisenstein were in mind, not Benjamin. Each of us went our own way in this; I who had been shocked into childish wonder somehow trawled up the shoe-box theatre from rainy days long ago, and started to draw up everything I could about my West London site – ideogramatically, not representationally – as if it were in a theatre.

The curtains came from David Hockney,[10] and were as sensually laden as were his. They twist and curl as if writhing under the import of the ideas with which they are inscribed, ideas that (in his words) 'hide something, or are about to reveal something'. The props drift in from Paul Klee sketches and the copses on hills came initially from Paul Nash landscapes, later from the sexualised watercolours of busty and butty hills by Ed Burra. Intellectual thinners were applied by acquaintance with the works of Ian Hamilton Finlay for whom, in my first architectural partnership, Kate Heron and I did the gallery at Stonypath in Lanarkshire, and also by a fascination with Shepherd and Jellicoe's line-drawn, bird's-eye view idealisations of great Italian gardens.[11]

I had seen the ideograms as leading to dialogues between designers and clients, avoiding the visitation upon others of a designer's own unconscious preferences. The ideograms led me to a collaboration with Graeme Hardie on an interactive modelling process in which shanty dwellers entering a self-build housing programme modelled their shanty on a board subdivided into squares – each of which represented the amount needed as a repayment on their loan on a new house which they later modelled on to the same board using some simple construction rules devised by architect Michael Lazenby. A thousand families were rehoused in this unusually empowering way before the success of the scheme made it so visible to authorities intent on slum clearance that it was blocked.[12]

Over the years the ideograms have developed a little, emphasising what is evident only in a few frames of the West London Project (it was set out like a storyboard for a film) – a frame in the shape of an idealised profile. This profile is there simply to remind us that

Leon van Schaik, ideogram concerning Allan Powell's TarraWarra Museum of Art (2004), included in the Melbourne Masters Architecture Exhibition at the Gallery. This architect, more than any other in Melbourne, is acutely conscious of his position in the culture, always looking over his shoulder, while on stage his 'dumb platonic solids' slide into a poetic alignment. © Leon van Schaik.

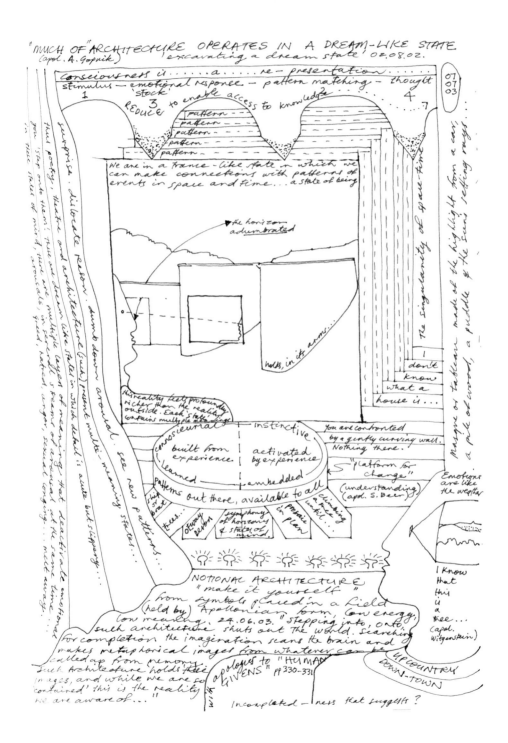

we are 'observers observing ourselves observing' and that we are surrounded by others doing the same thing at the same time.[13] Gordon Pask,[14] whose drawings explaining conversations are the most beguiling of diagrams, became an influence.

Here perhaps is the poetic of the ideogram: it is – as Frances Yates has it about the early Renaissance *teatro mundi* or 'memory theatre' – 'an aid for investigating the encyclopaedia and the world with the object of discovering new knowledge'.[15]

How do ideograms help in the discovery of new knowledge? Ideas, concepts and Eureka moments well up from the braided intelligences of beings, emotions and desires all tangled with lines of reason, and it takes time, daydreaming and reflection to bring them to a formulation that is simple and elegantly communicable.[16] I use ideograms to capture all of the floss in and around a topic on one page, and from this distillation I then move into the writing of an essay. I use them to encapsulate at critical moments the realisations of architects who are examining their own work in depth. I have tried using my theatres to capture the proceedings of a jury on an international urban design competition in Moscow, but the theatre of the room, one side peppered with oligarchs, proved too rich a mixture. An ideogram of these ideograms would be needed before an essay could emerge.

Mostly I think ideograms are a tool to open you to what you know, but don't know you know, and in that I echo the pragmatic advice of Tony Buzzan,[17] whose self-help booklets advise everyone that they can draw, and must draw to unlock their knowledge. He gets you to begin on a flat page; I suggest that you become three-dimensional, locating what you know spatially so that what is front of the mind does not preclude perspectives on what is on the periphery, what lies in the background, what is about to arrive on the stage: you create a theatre of your poetics, and connect these to those of others on the various horizons[18] that a theatre can suggest.

Notes

1   Le Corbusier and Pierre Jeaneret, 'What is America's Problem?', *Oeuvre Complète 1934–1938*, 2nd edn (Zurich), 1945, pp 61–3.
2   Alison and Peter Smithson, *Urban Structuring: Studies of Alison and Peter Smithson*, Studio Vista Reinhold Books (London/New York), 1967.
3   L van Schaik, 'Walls, toys and the ideal room: an analysis of the architecture of Sir John Soane', Mary Wall (ed), *AA Files* no 9, Architectural Association (London), 1985, pp 45–53.
4   S Steinberg, *Steinberg*, R Piper & Co/Verlag (Munich, Berlin), pp 148, 149.
5   London Tate Gallery, *Richard Hamilton*, exhibition catalogue (London), 1970, p 21.
6   Simon Sadler, *The Situationist City*, MIT Press (Cambridge, MA), 1998.
7   Bernard Tschumi and Nigel Coates, *The Discourse of Events: Themes 3*, Architectural Association (London), 1983.
8   Jenny Lowe, Nigel Coates, Doug Branson, Antoine Grumbach and Christian de Portzamparc, 'Chronicle in urban politics' in Bernard Tschumi (ed), *Chronicle in Urban Politics*, October 1973–June1974, Architectural Association (London), 1974.
9   Nigel Coates, *Ecstasy*, Architectural Association (London), 1992, still also wonderfully at it!
10   David Hockney (foreword by Mark Glazebrook), 'Curtain paintings', *Paintings, Prints and Drawings*

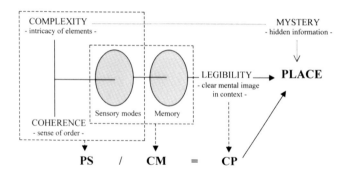

Figure 3 JM Malnar and F Vodvarka, Integrated Place Schematic, 2004. © Joy Monice Malnar and Frank Vodvarka.

In this construct, the theories of the Kaplans are brought to bear on our own explanation of perception as it occurs within a cultural context. Thus our perceptual systems are influenced by both prior experience as manifested in memory, and preference factors as they affect the perception of the contents of our milieu. Cultural modifiers are shaped by both culture and position in regard to context codes. In both diagrams, however, what are critical are the sensory modalities for the understanding of place. This importance is further emphasised when we combine the two diagrams to account for the effects of culture on both *how* we use our senses to understand spatial constructs, and the *contents* of the memory base used for comparison. Two aspects of this construct are apparent: first, that there is considerable interaction between perception and culture; and second, that sensory modalities are fundamental to both domains (figure 3).

We include this three-part progression to indicate the method we used to develop schematic diagrams relative to phenomenological design. Information is gathered from multiple sources – in the social and environmental sciences especially (where diagrams are usual) – and continuously added to existing schematics. Rather than using a 'list' format, we rely on a spatial 'feel' that indicates constant, dimensional interactions. That felt approach can, of course, be further refined. Charles W Rusch has created a diagram based on a functional model of mental processes. He suggests that awareness may have developed from the human need to reduce the sheer amount of information in the environment for survival. This entailed the 'filtering out' of less immediately vital material, and the concomitant 'structuring' of the remainder, ie giving it meaning.[8] Such 'recoding' of information is used to symbolise a large amount of detailed data, and leads to the ongoing process known as reflection.

Awareness, according to Rusch, assumes two forms: external awareness of the environment, and inner awareness, the attention paid to one's thoughts and bodily processes.[9] In his explanation of how sensory information from the environment enters human awareness, Rusch relies on Piaget's four-stage developmental model: the period of emotions, the sensory-motor period, the imaginal period and the period of formal operations. He notes that each period represents a phase of development during which

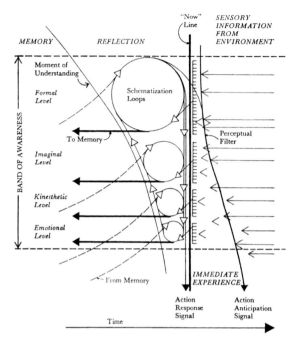

Figure 4 Charles W Rusch, Total Diagram: A Functional Model of Mental Process, 1970. © Charles W Rusch, Emeritus Professor of Architecture, University of Oregon.

we learn to 'structure' our experience, referring to objects and events encountered in our environment.[10] Finally, he maintains that through our immediate experience we absorb information from three sources: perception, conception and memory (figure 4).

Memory is especially vital, as it constantly recycles the information. Rusch says: 'The memory structure is by no means static or rigid; it is dynamic and constantly undergoing modification during recall when it is fed back through the constructive activity of immediate experience ... Thus, just as immediate experience is continuously changing, so also the memory structure is continuously being reconstituted.'[11] This theoretical framework has three implications: first, that it calls for an attitude which addresses the education of the whole mind; second, that it makes clear research issues surrounding environmental awareness by revealing the balance between the conceptual and perceptual; and third, that it helps elucidate a design process that relies on imagery as the medium of design thinking.[12]

There are still other diagrams that relate sensory information to human beings in a representational form. In *The Urban Stage*, A Richard Williams offers the reader a definition of the *sensory realm*: microenvironments – the smallest spatial components of the cultural/institutional fabric, or urban mosaic – as perception domains of all the senses: visual, tactile, sonic, thermal and olfactory.[13] Williams points out that designers have been trained to optimise form/function relationships that emphasise vision. 'Aside from meeting common standards of performance, architects do little creatively with acoustical, thermal, olfactory, and tactile sensory responses.'[14] His experience with

Figure 5 Richard Williams, Sensory Realm, 1980. Courtesy of A. Richard Williams, Tucson, Arizona.

theatrical performances, where organised sensory information is critical, suggests a new goal for architectural settings: 'to orchestrate and "tune" them over a full range of sensory responses, as flexibly as can be done on stage.'[15] His diagram relates sensations to the responsible senses, and to human sensibility (figure 5).

Perhaps the most interesting part of his diagram is that the human figure is present in spatial relationship to sensation. In fact, one of the most intriguing aspects of sensation is its range of reception and projection. It is this aspect of space that WH Auden refers to in his 'Prologue: The Birth of Architecture':

> Some thirty inches from my nose
> The frontier of my Person goes ...[16]

This raises the question of just how far our 'frontiers' actually do go. Reginald G Golledge and Robert J Stimson point out that, as the real world is complex, sending out millions of information signals, we can only be aware of a small portion of them. This information is experienced and recorded as differentials of colour, heat, motion, sound, pressure, direction or whatever else is present and within the range of the senses.[17] As we record only those stimuli that have a bearing on particular needs, perceptions may differ: 'The perceptions of two individuals vary as a function of differences in the content of the information presented and the differences in the ability of individuals to pick up the information messages.'[18] We illustrate the range of each sense by maintaining JJ Gibson's categories of the senses; that there is much overlap in their range suggests that which one takes precedence is unclear (figure 6).

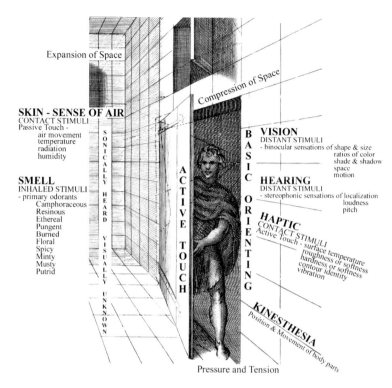

Figure 6 JM Malnar and F Vodvarka, Range of the Senses Chart, 2004. © Joy Monice Malnar and Frank Vodvarka.

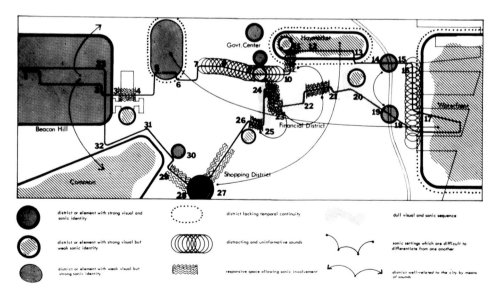

Figure 7 Michael Southworth, Evaluation of part of the Boston Soundscape, 1969. © Michael Southworth, 1969.

Concept and Reality

The role that the diagram is now playing in our attempts to theorise material reality in the late 20th century is not so different from the way the concept of the 'schema' was used by Kant to theorise Newtonian reality in the late 18th century. Both serve as synthetic explanatory devices (though no less real for that) that open up a space through which a perceptible reality may be related to the formal system that organises it, whether this latter is a priori or a posteriori as in the Kantian/Humian version. Another great thinker of the same era who ought not to be left out of consideration is Goethe, who, it can be argued, rejected the (apodictic) Kantian-Newtonian model in favour of a genetic interpretation of form. In brief, he placed his wager on the side of development, lodging the explanatory device in the space of abstract interactions taking place over time, so that form was always moving and represented only a visible, frozen section through a more fundamental organising logic that itself could be intuited, analytically described, but never actually held in the hands. Indeed Goethe is the father of the modern concept of diagram insofar as he insisted on formation as the locus of explanation, not appearance. This work can be found in all of Goethe's work on natural philosophy, on intuition, but most explicitly in his scientific writings, especially those on botany.

The relationship between perception, concept and reality is clearly related to the development of the schema concept of Kant. For Kant, the world of experience was divided into a 'material' and a 'formal' component. Material referred to sense-qualities found on the side of the object, the world, or, in the Kantian jargon, of the 'manifold'. The formal domain, that which we are interested in when we want to understand the diagram, belongs on the side of the perceiving mind or agent; it refers to an a priori organisation – this is Kant's Newtonian absoluteness speaking – a kind of engram or partitioning algorithm that lets sense experience – matter – enter into relation with itself to form higher level meanings and unities (I believe this to be the proto-origin of modern Gestalt theory). The formal, however, appears on the side of the subjective; it corresponds to the a priori schema which on its own is hollow, and must be filled in with data acquired from outside through the senses. For Kant, each term of the pair is inseparable from the other: subject and object, perception and reality, schema and senses. Otherwise the world collapses into shapeless abstraction or a senseless kaleidoscopic scattering. It was the task of the 20th-century neo-Kantians, and it is our task as well, to topologise the field of the encounter of each of the pair of terms. The neo-Kantian biologist Jakob Johann von Uexküll played an important role in doing this when he invented the concept of the *Umwelt*. The early Panofsky, on the other hand, showed how perspective played such a diagrammatic role in the formation of a cognitive, technological and aesthetic Gestalt, and Cassirer developed a theory of 'symbolic form' which again posits the work of a generative, topologising diagram that engenders both subject and object in any given context.

By using the word topology here I wish to introduce not only the shifting, connected meshwork in which form and matter play out their alternating struggle and their dance, but to insist that the diagram should not be understood as a reduction of the manifold, but a contraction, or, to use the medieval term, a complication of reality harbouring within itself the perpetual capacity to explicate or unfold. The diagram – or topologised schema – represents the plastic aspect of reality: subject and object can virtually masquerade as one another. This obviously poses a whole new set of problems and possibilities for the theory of perception, and it certainly frees us from static, vision-based concepts of space. Somewhere here, we've jettisoned both Newton and Kant, even though they served as the primary ladders to our modern position.

We might say they emit formative and organisational influence that cannot help but be 'embodied' in all subsequent states of the given region of concrete reality in which it is placed.[1] But this represents a very complex play of hybridisation and creolisation because every component of what I have called concrete reality is itself the expression of many other previous diagrams that have only temporarily been resolved (or 'tested', as in an experiment) and lodged in form. The view of reality that I have always tried to foster in my work (and which I like to believe that I am drawing from Nietzsche) is precisely one in which the play of form is seen as a perpetual communication of moduluses, or impetuses – generating centres – which we are here agreeing to call diagrams. It is my view that these are fundamentally geometric in nature, but when I use the word geometry I of course am referring to the modern, non-Euclidean or 'rubber sheet' variety that deals with transitions and their logic … Diagrams then are active, and the view that sees them as mere blueprints to be translated or reproduced is outdated. The diagram is the engine of novelty, good as well as ill.

Abstract Machines
… It is worth pointing out though that the diagram concept functions in Foucault's book [*Discipline and Punish*] as if it, itself, were a diagram.[2] In other words, it functions as an embedded entity, separate yet indissociable from the concrete work-event (the book and system of concepts known as *Surveiller et punir*) that it animates and in which it resides. So how then do you isolate a diagram from the concrete events it generates? This is where Deleuze[3] has made his contribution to the problem, by identifying the diagram with a class of phenomena that he calls abstract machines. Abstract machines are precisely what they claim to be: they are abstract because conceptually and ontologically distinct from material reality yet they are fully functioning machines nonetheless, that is, they are agencies of assemblage, organisation and deployment … The argument, stated simply, is as follows: to every organised entity there corresponds a microregime of forces that endows it with its general shape and programme. Every object is a composition of forces, and the compositional event is the work or expression of an abstract machine. What I call the 'conductivity hypothesis' is a major component of some mathematical work being done these days as well as work in the biological sciences. It states that

abstract machines, or organised shaping forces, or micromorphological regimes, are themselves part of larger assemblages, larger abstract machines through which they communicate as if across a single continuum. Events in one place transmit their effects and successes to other places, and indeed to other scales … Fields are one of the models with which scientists explain the incidents of influence that we are here agreeing by convention to call diagrams. There arise particular problems, of course, when one is careless in developing models to explain how remote events, or events separated in time rather than space are related (such as in the work of Rupert Sheldrake) but history is full of provocative non-metaphysical models to explain such phenomena as well. I bring this all up because I like to claim that what we are dealing with here is simultaneously a new type of materialism (as Foucault called it, 'un materialisme de l'incorporel') and a kind of neo-vitalism. It calls for a new epistemology of action and event, and sees forms and things as mere chimeras of these underlying diagrammatic processes. Politics must become the politics of the diagram and history must be seen as the history of diagrammatic life, not merely of the forms it threw up.

Approaching the incorporeal is one of the major challenges of contemporary design practice. There were times – more innocent times to be sure – when this was done with very little self-consciousness and with sweeping brilliance; one thinks of the work of Moholy-Nagy, the Constructivists, certain filmmakers from Eisenstein to Kubrick, Buckminster Fuller, Robert Smithson, the aesthetico-philosophical urbanist movements of the late 1950s and 1960s, etc. They seemed instinctively to understand their role as intermediaries and had a clear intuition of the interstitial space that they had to occupy to become diagrammatists … In biology one is quite at ease discussing the distinct domains of genotype (where data is encoded in a four-letter language of rudimentary instructions) and phenotype (the marvellously rich world of novel shapes and their concatenations), and, with a bit more strain, of an intermediary space that links the two and where regulatory processes guide the first into the second. It would already be something for designers to adopt the 'mechanistic genetic' position and conceive of a genotypic diagrammatism as underlying all phenotypic or formal expression. And yet, I will always insist that the diagram lies in the space between the two, in the wild field of cybernetic interactions (what Deleuze, after Bergson, has called actualisation), regulatory pressures and channels, and control loops. Thus, once again, one misunderstands the diagram when one conceives of it as a template rather than as a flow.

The Incorporeal
This is where the problem of diagrammatism takes on its post-war configuration. After the Second World War there was an extraordinary increase in the belief and application of science and engineering to everyday life, which brought along an increasing application of invisible material logics to explain and generate reality … the advent of controlled nuclear processes, microwave and radar signal processing, industrial applications of synthetic chemistry, ballistics and cryptology were almost entirely made

possible by both theoretical and practical advances in information science. Industrial societies became increasingly saturated with these new embedded logics and the corresponding motor habits that they produced, but they became subjugated by them invisibly, according to what one could call a 'subtle coup'. The diagram is now very usefully understood as informational. At present the sciences of complexity give us the most useful understanding of the dynamic, algorithmic nature of diagrams. Complexity theory can be said to target three primary phenomena in the natural and the non-natural world: integration, organisation and coordination. These phenomena undeniably exist in the world, but science has never been able to interrogate these phenomena in their customary numerical or 'hard' terms. Philosophy has always had to step in, along with some makeshift methods in the social sciences and occasionally aesthetics. When we, today, enquire into the nature and activity of the diagram we are asking: 'When something appears, what agencies are responsible for giving this particular shape to this particular appearance?' Complexity theory, or dynamical systems theory, is seeking to reconfigure the answer to this question by positing the perpetual interaction of moving, evolving systems: one invisible (the diagram) and one visible (the real). The primary phenomena studied by the new sciences are actually visible to, or intuitable by, a living observer, but not to a non-living one, say to a camera or a measuring device …

Next would be the phenomenon of organisation. Organisation played a central role in the life sciences in the 1920s and 1930s and then again in the 1960s to address the philosophical impasses that still carried over from the older mechanist-vitalist debates … Organisation relies on the notion of pattern, it attempts to explain how patterns can arise uniquely through internal controls, and how these control factors sustain themselves, take on a direction, and then assume the appearance of autonomy, or life. The concept of organisation targets primarily the emergence of sequenced events as the source of developmental mechanics and formal stability. These were exactly the questions that Foucault was asking about history at an institutional and discursive level …

Indeed complexity is the movement towards biology (some might say towards emergent intelligence, though forms of intelligence are around us everywhere, which is why we postulate the concept of the diagram as a regulatory or generative mechanism). It marks the transition where communication, control and pattern formation – in a single phrase, relationships of information – take over in an organised substrate from relationships of energy. Historically, this movement – the emergence of what I like to call a 'bio-logic' – began with the 19th century's science of heat (thermodynamics) as the study of ineluctable transitions (cold to hot, order to disorder, difference to homogeneity) and the theory of evolution (the homogenous and simple, to the differentiated and the complex). The life sciences could not fully emerge on an independent basis until a theoretical-mathematical basis could be provided for them. Physics itself had to become an 'information' science before biology could emerge gradually to supplant it. (This history goes from Boltzmann's statistical theory of gases to the post-war era's elaborations by

Virtual London, survey of air pollution by the Centre for Advanced Spatial Analysis, UCL, 2007. Diagram from the digital model of London. © Image courtesy of the Centre for Advanced Spatial Analysis (CASA), University College London and the Governmental Research Group, Kings College London.

Design Director: Tibor Kalman (American, born Hungary, 1949–99). Designer: Marlene McCarty (American, born 1957). Postcard: Restaurant Florent: Mirth (typography/table), 1989. Firm: M & co., 1979–93. Client: Florent Morellet. This blurring of the distinctions between drawing, diagram, typography, graphic design, text/list and annotation creates not just a design for an interior and a set of products but includes programme, atmosphere, mood, social relations, emotions and multisensory and stylistic information with an exceptional economy and originality of means. © Cooper-Hewitt, National Design Museum, Smithsonian Institution. Gift of Tibor Kalman/ M & co., 1993-151-281.

Stan Allen, Field Conditions Diagrams, 1985. © Courtesy of Stan Allen.

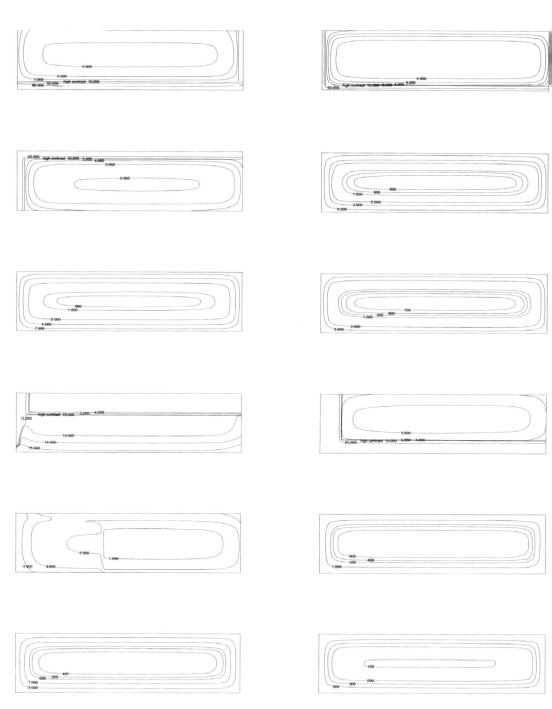

New Novartis Pharma Headquarters competition, Basel. Lighting diagrams. *Above*: Lux fields and gradients. *Opposite*: Summer (upper rows) and winter (lower rows) solstice diagrams of natural daylighting (during cloudy and clear weather) illumination levels.

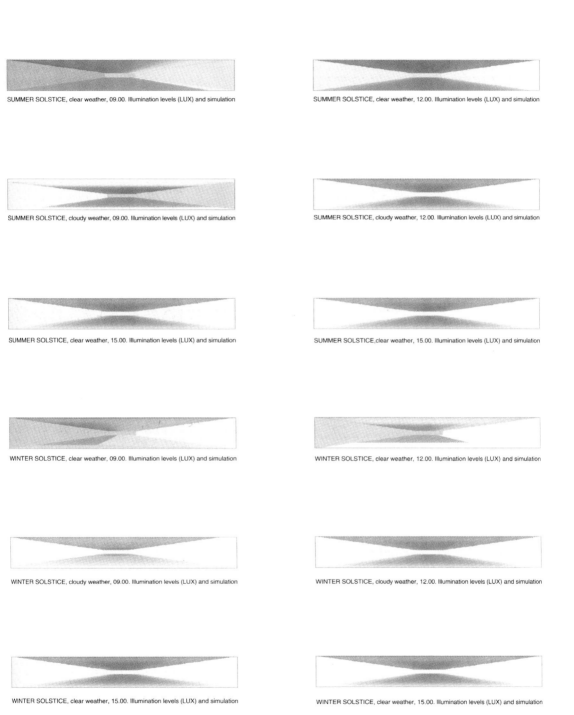

SUMMER SOLSTICE, clear weather, 09.00. Illumination levels (LUX) and simulation

SUMMER SOLSTICE, clear weather, 12.00. Illumination levels (LUX) and simulation

SUMMER SOLSTICE, cloudy weather, 09.00. Illumination levels (LUX) and simulation

SUMMER SOLSTICE, cloudy weather, 12.00. Illumination levels (LUX) and simulation

SUMMER SOLSTICE, clear weather, 15.00. Illumination levels (LUX) and simulation

SUMMER SOLSTICE,clear weather, 15.00. Illumination levels (LUX) and simulation

WINTER SOLSTICE, clear weather, 09.00. Illumination levels (LUX) and simulation

WINTER SOLSTICE, clear weather, 12.00. Illumination levels (LUX) and simulation

WINTER SOLSTICE, cloudy weather, 09.00. Illumination levels (LUX) and simulation

WINTER SOLSTICE, cloudy weather, 12.00. Illumination levels (LUX) and simulation

WINTER SOLSTICE, clear weather, 15.00. Illumination levels (LUX) and simulation

WINTER SOLSTICE, clear weather, 15.00. Illumination levels (LUX) and simulation

SANAA's concern for the architectural phenomenology of ephemeral light and form effects is demonstrated in this project through its simultaneously scientific and poetic, experiential concern for architectural affects designed using diagrams. © SAANA.

Diagramming the Interior

Mark Taylor

Mark Taylor's new essay assesses the impact of the diagram on interior design from the late 19th century to the present. Taylor identifies the pop-cultural discourse of advice writing in both books and magazines as a starting point for his analysis. Drawing on diverse sources, his analysis focuses on texts relating to the dynamics of use and flexibility by Catherine Beecher, Harriet Beecher Stowe, Melusina Fay Peirce, Mary Haweis and Christine Frederick among others. The examples in these texts use the home, domestic housekeeping and kitchens as the sites and practices of intervention through which interior design innovations can be enacted. Taylor's analysis identifies the innovations in both the social and the political aspects of space and the critique of static space behind these seemingly amateurish and innocuous texts. Identifying these contributions as early precursors of Modernism's open-plan and flexible, dynamic spaces, Taylor also interprets them with a critical concern for the oppositions and hierarchies that can exist in spatial design, and which are the hallmarks of recent Postmodern, phenomenological approaches to interior design and its theorisations. The progressive and subversive 'paradigms for living' implicit in these diagrams can be argued to present a model of greater economic, social and political equality as well as representing a more balanced set of power relations in the home. Progressing through the 20th century to the present, Taylor's analysis shifts beyond the dressed body and on to the more intimate rituals of the revealed body to further examine how diagrams of the interior, and the interior as a set of diagrams, are also mediators, sites and grounds for the design of social and sexual intimacy. Through a consideration of the link between design, identity and intimacy (whether of the invisible, fashioned or sexualised body), the diagrams of interiors are reconfigured as radical and critical tools for an animate, material and emancipatory 'redressing' of the balance between the body, identity, sexuality, gender, function, (mis)use, aesthetics and the interior.

The interior is subject to diagramming in many guises often devised by architects concerned with social occupations or efficiencies in structuring and organising space. Their results, including adjacency relations, bubble diagrams and so on, are well documented and tend to influence perceptions and practice of interior design. However, there exists another legacy that concerns interior design's emergence and professionalisation through advice writing and a specific engagement with the morphology of body and space as lived and practised.

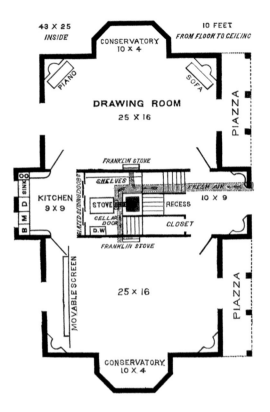

Catherine Beecher and Harriet Beecher Stowe, *The American Woman's Home*, 1869. Plan of the first floor presents a new geometry of living situating female dominance squarely on the home. Copyright and courtesy of Mount Holyoke College Archives and Special Collections.

In their seminal publication *The American Woman's Home* (1869), Catherine Beecher and Harriet Beecher Stowe published a drawing titled 'The Ground Plan of the First Floor'.[1] At first glance it reads like any period plan drawing that includes dimensions, wall openings and stairs except for the indication of three pieces of furniture and a detailed layout for the kitchen. Located opposite the entrance and behind the stair, the centrally positioned kitchen enables the fireplace flue to occupy the centre of the plan.

This new geometry of living is presented by the Beechers as 'a mode of economizing time, labor, and expense by the close packing of conveniences'. To some extent this drawing discloses a spatial politics through the intersection of 'programme' and 'inhabitation'. First, the drawing transforms or disrupts traditionally static horizontal space through the appropriation of lines that define fields of activity as much as they resemble conventional proximity indicators. For example, a line described as 'movable screen' suggests that fluidity of activity is maintained by the repositioning of the 'wardrobe' concealing beds and dressing areas. Transcending fixed space, this floor-to-ceiling furniture piece indicates a mobile relationship between use and activity. Diagrammed this way, it is an early sign that the relationship between interiors and the inhabiting subject is not static and extends beyond loose furniture and accessories. Moreover, Penny Sparke reaffirms that 'the constantly transforming nature of the domestic interior is such that neither it, nor the identities it represents, can ever be stable'.[2]

Second, as advocates of domestic feminism, the Beechers in their writing/drawing mark another shift in thinking about the designed interior. As a specific disciplinary device, the drawing situates female 'dominance' squarely on the home in order to undo or disturb traditional aesthetic ordering devices. However, in architectural resolution this 'diagram' may be insufficient by our current understanding of the term. That is, it may (as drawn) resemble a new paradigm for living rather than impart a self-generating or self-organising process, particularly when the diagram is regarded as operating between conventional plan and accompanying text.

The Beechers' account marks a shift in thinking about the designed interior that is found in other writers of the period. For example, Dolores Hayden observes that Melusina Fay Peirce's radical change to domestic organisation includes a description of the requirements for a cooperative housekeeping association.[3] This and other proposals for simplified kitchenless houses are diagrams that register political and social change.[4] They attempt to replace the 'neutral', objective nature of geometrical descriptions with alternative landscapes in which women's visibility is central. Mediating between words and form, they reframe architecture through progressive economic and egalitarian ideals. To some extent Peirce declares both a social and a disciplinary project, a condition Somel indicates is present when 'working diagrammatically', suggesting it is found 'not by representing a particular condition, but by subverting dominant oppositions and hierarchies currently constitutive of the discourse'.[5]

Other 19th century writers focusing on dismantling object-based interiors include the art critic and enfranchisement campaigner Mary Haweis (1848–98). Rather than formalise any vision for constructing architecture as a tectonic or mathematical imperative, she turns to the wider discursive fields of material culture and domestic decorative strategies

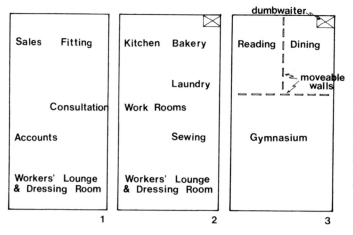

Diagrammatic plan of Melusina Fay Peirce's Cooperative Housekeeping Society. From Dolores Hayden, *The Grand Domestic Revolution*, 1981. Working diagrammatically, Peirce declares both a social and disciplinary project. © MIT Press from the book by Dolores Hayden *The Grand Domestic Revolution*, 1981, p 70.

as a framework for understanding spatial relations between body and interior. More particularly, she uses 'dress' to index a process in which the activity of 'dressing' is both thing and process. Given her particular interest in women's occupation of the domestic realm, a connection between interior spaces, women and the body opens an ambiguity whereby the interior is both a projection of the body and a carefully constructed setting for the presentation of 'beauty's worth'.[6]

Understood as a mirroring of the body or a projection of the domestic body into its environment, surroundings become an extension of self achieved by 'carefully decorating our rooms as a background to our figures'.[7] To pacify the inevitable backlash from a literalist interpretation of artistic intent, she argues that dress becomes the first outward projection and that wall ornamentation is another, evidenced by the idea that people do not adapt to their walls but that 'their walls are to be adapted to them'.[8] In other words, this slight shift in emphasis is designed to undermine the conventional room-by-room analysis and style-based decorative conventions, in order to transform the discourse from within.

Although Haweis's writing is replete with the taxonomy of a Victorian amateur, and lacks any drawn referent beyond pictorial illustration, there is a shift from the advice writers' concern with aesthetic qualities towards a diagrammatic understanding of relationships between body (female) and space (home). The intention it seems is not to decorate in response to any existing architectural ordering devices, but to dress the surrounding environment by unfolding or extending from the body. This general argument is conceptually distinct from practice a century earlier, which according to Robin Evans was when 'furniture occupies the room and then the figures inhabit the furniture'.[9] Such privileging of inanimate forms as spatial and material ordering devices has been expressed by others. For example, the writer Edgar Allen Poe in *Philosophy of Furniture* (1840) remarks that 'the soul of the apartment is the carpet ... from it are deduced not only the hues but the forms of all objects incumbent.'[10]

By the early 20th century some thoughts on spatial organisation had repositioned body-centred spatial strategies through ideas of efficiency and functionality. Christine Frederick, the self-titled 'household efficiency engineer', constructed a critique of the kitchen through analyses of operational processes, and argued for equipment placement to follow the actual order of work.[11] In *The New Housekeeping* (1914), her kitchen analysis is conducted through the 'ideal' way to prepare food, offering a description of the processes involved in making an omelette.[12] Her functional diagrams of the two kitchen processes – preparing and clearing away – are represented as 'efficient grouping of kitchen equipment' and 'badly grouped kitchen equipment'.[13] Moreover, they use arrows and lines as representations of movement and flow that are in stark contrast to similar representations in her later volume, *Household Engineering* (1923), where the original diagram is transposed to resemble a conventional plan drawing.[14]

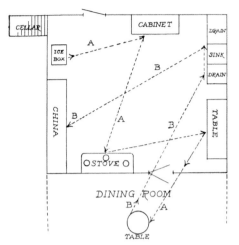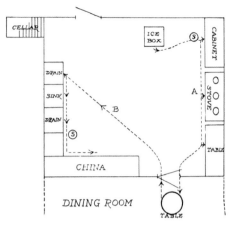

Diagram showing badly arranged equipment, which makes confused intersecting chains of steps, in either preparing or clearing away a meal. (A — preparing; B — clearing)

Diagram showing proper arrangement of equipment, which makes a simple chain of steps, in either preparing or clearing away a meal. (A — preparing; B — clearing)

Christine Frederick, *The New Housekeeping*, 1914. Functional diagram of the kitchen process. From the Heath Collection, Albert R Mann Library, Cornel University, 2008. © Albert R Mann Library, Cornell University, 2008.

Returning to questions of the decorative interior, Dorothy Todd and Raymond Mortimer in *The New Interior Decoration* (1929) again raise the notion that the adorned interior is some form of 'projection'. Following a quasi-anthropological argument, they suggest that for prehistoric humans the need to adorn shelters was a powerful impulse, 'second only to the desire to adorn our own bodies'.[15] By associating adornment with personality, they conclude, like others, that homes are 'a projection of ourselves' and a place where 'we see the facets of our character mirrored in the objects with which we have surrounded ourselves'.

Such propositional writing expresses a set of spatial relations through a series of statements that are to some extent 'thought images' even though they are yet to be translated through visual thinking. As abstractions, they substitute one dominant discourse for another that Beverly Gordon identifies through a gendered history of the interior, confirming that the 19th-century bourgeois interior was one of the few locations available for women's self-expression – an expression that is categorised as the conceptual conflation of women and interiors.[16] Working diagrammatically, she suggests that body and interior space are interchangeable, citing several examples that affirm women's bodies as an important ornamental factor in decorating a room. Moreover, she notes that remnants of this conflation metaphor still abound, with many examples indicating that concerns are articulated in a manner that transcends the idea of advice writing per se. For example, Debora Silverman, writing in *Art Nouveau in Fin-de-Siecle France* (1989), observes that it was the Goncourts who 'clarified how the rococo interior was inseparable from its female identity'.[17]

Although much of this writing is concerned with gender identification, questions of sexuality and the interior shift the diagram, raising a different relationship of the body to the interior. For example, Lee Edelman's 'queer theory' reading of a public men's room in a fashionable New York bar recognises Foucault's notion that architecture and sexuality are inextricably linked because architecture houses sexualised beings. Edelman argues that the men's room is an environment that is constructed (made/given rise to) by men's behaviour in the space, and at the same time cultural/social actions are conditioned by the space itself.[18] He suggests that such spaces are far from any neutral, technological response to bodily necessities, but are designed by, and have designs on, men. Though diagrams do not appear in his text, and it is primarily concerned with social and psychological engagement of space, Edelman anticipates changes to the diagramming of body/space relations, particularly as architecture is used to condition space when male sexuality is challenged by cultural norms of sexually specific behaviour.

One design project that contributes to this debate is 'Ken's Gym' by Byron Kinnaird and Richard Burns.[19] Initially Kinnaird and Burns attempted to destabilise the conventionality of the male changing-room through the study of behaviour and actions conditioned by same-sex desire. Diagramming an alternative to the 'neutral' hygienic, functional environment, they responded to particular bodily relations and, in Edelman's terms, culturally abjected bodily functions. This included a reorganisation of conventional layout so that to enter the shower/display room participants have to step over the 'piss wall' floor drain. Moreover, in a bid to challenge the cultural regulation of desire, they produced alternative anthropometric data derived from a study of sexual activity in the men's changing-room. Here architecture, masculinity and sexuality are interlinked and the functional diagram becomes a sexual diagram.

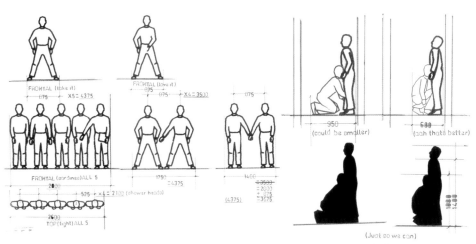

left: Byron Kinnaird, Frontal Series Test, 2005. The functional becomes sexual when same-sex desire and bodily relations are diagrammed as alternate anthropometric data.
right: Byron Kinnaird, Sectional Shower Test, 2005. © Byron Kinnaird with Richard Burns.

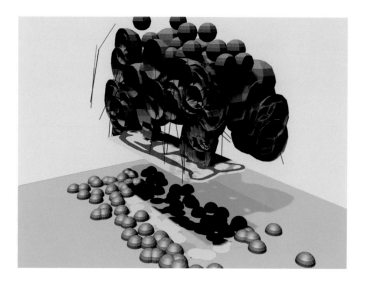

Matthew Randell, diagram of the Full Body Massage Suite, 2006. This digital diagram anticipates the sensuality of a semi-naked body and the intimacy between form and material. © Matthew Randell, Diana Chaney and Yi Wen Seow.

More recently, digital technologies have allowed increasingly sophisticated spatial renderings, but also facilitate three- and four-dimensional modelling that advances surface as the structuring principle of architecture. Andrew Benjamin, writing in *Armed Surfaces* (2004), suggests that Dagmar Richter understands the computer-generated surface as a diagram in which 'the diagram allows for specific modes of investigation'.[20] Careful to avoid construing the diagram volumetrically, Richter's contextual models for the Dom-in(f)o House engage dialectics of inside and outside, structure and surface, and so on. However, these prototypes are form-generational as abstractions, whereas the Full Body Massage suite by Chaney, Randell and Seow diagrams the masseur's interaction with the client, spatialising the dynamics of the activity.[21] In this process a number of constraints are established, including registering the body's movement in space during massage, and mapping changes when boundaries extend. The three-dimensional digital diagram informed by occupational activity defines tolerance volumes and material arrangement, anticipating the sensuality of the semi-naked body and intimacy between form and materials as a dynamic morphology.

Part of what is demonstrated here is that by redistributing functions the diagram, rather than representing concepts and objects external to architecture, retains an instrumental role, resolute with inherent abstract potentials. That is, it reprogrammes space relative to specific rather than general attributes, opening the interior to investigation in a political sense. With the focus on the gendered, sexed and raced performative body, particular activities, occupations and events provide a data field in which connections supplant traditions, and the diagram's architectural resolution is not its extrusion. Moreover, while I have focused on the interior as a spatial extension of the body manifested through material elements, there is disclosed a relationship between the animate and the material, and the diagrammatic and the representational, that is particular to the discourse of the interior.

Notes

1   Catharine E Beecher and Harriet Beecher Stowe, *The American Woman's Home: or Principles of Domestic Science; Being A Guide to the Formation and Maintenance of Economical, Healthful, Beautiful, and Christian Homes*, JB Ford and Company (New York), 1869, p 26.
2   Penny Sparke, Introduction, Susie McKellar and Penny Sparke (eds), *Interior Design and Identity*, Manchester University Press (Manchester), 2004, p 2.
3   Dolores Hayden, *The Grand Domestic Revolution: A History of Feminist Designs for American Homes, Neighborhoods, and Cities*, MIT Press (Cambridge, MA), 1981, pp 69, 72.
4   Dolores Hayden, *The Grand Domestic Revolution*, MIT Press pp 70–1.
5   RE Somel, Introduction, Peter Eisenman, *Diagram Diaries*, Rizzoli (New York), 1999, p 23.
6   See Mary Haweis, *The Art of Beauty*, Chatto and Windus (London), 1878, and Mary Haweis, *The Art of Decoration*, Chatto and Windus (London), 1881.
7   Mary Haweis, *The Art of Beauty*, p 194.
8   Mary Haweis, *The Art of Decoration*, p 23.
9   Robin Evans, *Translations from Drawing to Building and Other Essays*, Architectural Association (London), 1997, p 219.
10 Edgar Allen Poe, *Philosophy of Furniture*, ReadBook On Line.net http://www.readbookonline.net/readOnLine/518/ (accessed 18 August 2006).
11 Christine Frederick published the outcome of her studies in several places including *Ladies Home Journal*, 13 September, 20 October, 19 November and 16 December 1912.
12 Christine Frederick, *The New Housekeeping: Efficient Studies in Home Management*, Doubleday (New York), 1914, p 51.
13 Christine Frederick, *The New Housekeeping*, p 52.
14 Christine Frederick, *Household Engineering: Scientific Management in the Home*, American School of Home Economics (Chicago), 1923.
15 Dorothy Todd and Raymond Mortimer, *The New Interior Decoration: An Introduction to its Principles, and International Survey of its Methods*, Scribner's (New York), 1929, p 1. Between 1922 and 1926 Dorothy Todd was the editor of British *Vogue*, to which the literary and art critic Raymond Mortimer was a contributing writer.
16 Beverly Gordon, 'Woman's domestic body: the conceptual conflation of women and interiors in the industrial age', *Winterthur Portfolio*, vol 31 no 4, 1996, pp 281–301.
17 Debora Silverman, *Art Nouveau in Fin-de-Siecle France: Politics, Psychology, and Style*, University of California Press (Berkeley), 1989, p 27.
18 Lee Edelman, 'Men's Room' in Joel Sanders (ed), *Stud: Architectures of Masculinity*, Princeton Architectural Press (New York), 1996, p 152.
19 This project was conducted at Victoria University Wellington, New Zealand. Studio director Mark Taylor. Student project, 'Ken's Gym'. Students Ken Tang (concept), Byron Kinnaird and Richard Burns (developed design).
20 See Dagmar Richter, *Armed Surfaces*, Black Dog Publishing (London), 2004.
21 This project was conducted at Victoria University Wellington, New Zealand. Studio directors, Mark Taylor and Mark Burry. Student project 'Full Body Massage Suite'. Students Yijing-xu (concept), Diana Chaney, Matthew Randell and Yi Wen Seow (developed design).

Diagrams in Landscape Architecture

Jacky Bowring and Simon Swaffield

Using examples drawn from the American Midwest, Australia and Europe, Associate Professor Jacky Bowring and Professor Simon Swaffield (Lincoln University, New Zealand) consider, in this newly commissioned essay, the use of the diagram in the discipline and practice of landscape design. They explore its possible limits and its graphic languages in capturing a range of critical landscape and design phenomena in analysis and imagination, past and future. Exercising caution, they point to the ways in which diagrams, as design representations, themselves 'shape' the results. They pay particular attention to the phenomenological, emotive, multisensory, subjective experience of landscape design and point out the ways in which these resist diagrammatic representation and reduction. For Bowring and Swaffield, the organic, fluid, self-organising and self-regenerating living materials and systems of landscape impose a series of unique challenges in the representation of its design. Their ontological and epistemological problematisation of the experience and nature of landscape challenges the ability of both the designer and the diagram to deal with the particular and ephemeral nature of landscape, its site specificity, the temporal, ecological cycles of sedimentation and erosion and its proprietary materiality. As interfaces of human and ecological materials and processes, landscape diagrams are necessarily forced into dealing with contingent, evolving, emergent and highly unstable and uncertain 'open' systems. Using examples from Frederick Law Olmsted, Lawrence Halprin, Kevin Lynch, Bernard Tschumi, James Corner, Anuradha Mathur, Terry Harkness and Dilip Da Cunha, Bowring and Swaffield conclude with a consideration of the effects of new digital technologies and computational techniques on new forms of diagram developed as a response to the challenges they have set out. They note that despite the increasing ability of diagram technologies as simulacra of process, they are only as good as the creative intelligences behind them.

Landscape architecture faces an unusual set of challenges in the way it uses diagrams. The first is the dynamic quality of landscape as a medium. Landscapes are fluid and organic, self-organising and self-regenerating. They are continually in flux – literally alive. Designed landscapes are therefore never complete – they grow, and mature, and decay. Design and planning diagrams in landscape architecture must therefore embrace the temporality of diurnal, seasonal and life cycles; of sedimentation and erosion, of life and death.

Another challenge arises from the range of scales at which landscape architecture engages with the phenomenal complexity of the world. It must address the selection and management of individual plants, as well as plant associations, ecosystems and the wider landscape mosaic.[1] Landscape design shapes the way that natural and man-made materials combine and interface, and design and planning interventions reconfigure individual sites, precincts, neighbourhoods and the green infrastructure of whole cities, while landscape assessment and policy extends to the regional, national and even global scale. Landscape diagrams must therefore be multiscalar, capable of unfolding into many levels of understanding and application.

Landscape architecture is a profoundly phenomenological enterprise, and its most compelling and significant achievements are often intangible, experiential and multi-sensory. So diagrams must also capture the ephemeral, and the transient. Perhaps for this reason diagrams in landscape architecture are always moments in time – a crystallisation of complex dynamics expressed in a graphic gesture.

Finally, landscape architecture is a profoundly social process, rich in both human creativity and in misunderstanding. Landscape – in its original form as *landschaft* – was a social phenomenon, a way of managing the world,[2] and this sense of landscape as agency is again gaining ascendancy in the discipline.[3] Diagrams that communicate understanding, intention and possibility are therefore integral to the way that landscape architecture engages with wider society and culture.

Landscape architects use diagrams to make sense of this complexity, both as analytical tools and as generative expressions of design imaginings. The choice of diagrammatic paradigm and style shapes and filters the infinite richness of the phenomenal world – in all its dimensions – into a realm of possibility, a 'site' for design intention and action.[4] Each diagram is therefore a schema – a representational analogue – of the designer's own conception of the world, a microcosm of *their* discipline.

In this contribution we briefly explore the way that diagrams are used within landscape architecture to analyse and imagine, and to consider both past and future. We also examine the limitations and challenges of diagrammatic representation. The focus is upon the modern discipline of the 20th century, as space precludes a more comprehensive historical survey, and for similar reasons the emphasis is upon the Western, largely English-speaking world.

Diagramming the landscape

Diagrams are a means of simplifying or conceptualising, and are distinguished by their abstraction, but they have to remain visually accessible in order to be useful. Like metaphors,[5] diagrams 'carry' ideas into another form, and the process of abstraction can involve a leap of faith in terms of comprehension. The London Underground map is a classic example of such a shift, in the way it moves beyond the orthodox notational systems of mapping into an abstract, yet still accessible, diagram. Each landscape architecture diagram has to make a similar transformation as it traces a course through the complexity of time and space to graphically represent an idea that can be readily grasped. Any graphic depiction of landscape involves such processes of transformation, whether into conventional forms of notation such as sketches, as multimedia artistic expressions or even through text.

James Corner has argued that representation is both analytical and generative,[6] and diagrams express this dual function. Analytical diagrams play an organisational role in design, through explaining the genesis of a landscape, site or project, by depicting its contemporary conditions or relationships, and by projecting the intended future of the site through extrapolation of the design intervention. Elizabeth Meyer has pointed out the way that the early shapers of the landscape architecture profession in North America during the 19th century, such as Frederick Law Olmsted, were highly sensitised to the specific nature of each site – its geology, geomorphology and ecology – and used a range of graphical devices to articulate site qualities.[7] That diagrammatic attention to the material genesis of landscape is still expressed in modern and contemporary practice, and is exemplified in Ian McHarg's ecological design method,[8] with the so-called 'sieving' approach which used layered analysis of existing conditions to derive a cumulative suitability map as the basis for design and planning intervention. Figure 1 illustrates the process in analogue form. Today, much of this analysis is digital, yet the process of graphical abstraction remains essentially the same.

Figure 1 'Layered Sieve',
© Jacky Bowring.

Analytical diagrams of ecological process can also be used to express future intentions for the management of the living landscape. A notable feature of modern Dutch landscape architecture has been its careful manipulation of plant succession, characterised by a diagramming technique in which the designer's intentions for changing species composition of different landscape zones are projected into the future. A recent application can be seen in the diagrams prepared by the practice Field Operations for *Fresh Kills*, an extensive landscape project on the former landfill site on Staten Island, New York. These show prospective analyses of stages in the intended transformation of the ecology of the site (figure 2).

As we note below, representation of human experience of landscape pushes the limits of diagrammatic technique. However, the cumulative experience of movement along prescribed paths or routes can be distilled into diagrams. Kevin Lynch's classic diagrams of city form[9] and the 'view from the road'[10] are examples of the way analytical diagrams have been used to make sense of complex movement and perception in space and time. Once captured in an abstract diagram, the concepts become the basis for analysis of design possibilities. The diagrammatic 'language' of edge, node, district and landmark developed by Lynch to summarise the way people experience the urban fabric has become embedded in landscape architectural education and practice at multiple scales, as well as informing landscape ecology.[11]

Diagrams are also generative tools – agents of investigation and revelation, forming the armatures on which ideas can condense. Through expressing or reformulating ideas, diagrams can open things out in a way that allows for a transcending or subverting of the status quo, as a means of generation in design. As well as their pragmatic strengths in communication, diagrams also have poetic potential through their ability to create new associations, to excavate affinities, to become vehicles for discovery. Figures 3, 4 and 5 illustrate the conceptual potency of generative diagramming. All three employ the idea of the 'layer' to first separate, and then recombine, complexity. While the idea of the layer echoes the legacy of McHarg's suitability sieving, in these examples the strategy of the layer generates the design itself, and the diagrams are, in effect, an abbreviated expression of design process.

In 'Gardens from Region', Terry Harkness analyses the character of regional landscapes in the Midwest to create typologies, which he then uses to generate design responses (figure 3). In contrast, Bernard Tschumi's iconic diagram for Parc de la Villette in Paris (figure 4) layers abstract patterns of points, lines and surfaces, derived from a conceptual geometric analysis. The layers are brought together in an arbitrary juxtaposition in the final park, subverting – or deconstructing – a conventional park design process. A third perspective on the process of recombination is found in the layers that are sedimented together to generate Room 4.1.3's Garden of Australian Dreams in Canberra, Australia. These are primarily content driven. Layers of maps showing such wide-ranging topics as

existing habitats ————————→ ————————→

| YEAR | 1 | 2 | 3 | 4 | 5 | 6 | 7 | 8 | 9 | 10 | 11 | 12 | 13 | 14 | 15 |

GRASSLAND
STRIP CROPPING

Strip cropping is an industrial-scale technique for increasing the organic content of poor soils, chelating metals and toxins (inhibiting their uptake by plants), increasing soil depth, controlling weeds and increasing aeration.

A crop rotation system is proposed to improve the existing topsoil cover without importing large quantities of new soil.

The cultivated soils will support native prairie and meadow. In the wetter areas of the mounds, shallow-rooted successional woodland will ultimately diversify the grassland biotopes.

NORTH AND SOUTH MOUNDS west face 130 acres

| CROP A ROWS | | ESTABLISH NATIVE PRAIRIE | | ALLOW SUCCESSIONAL WOODLAND ON WET AREAS, MOW D... |
| CROP B ROWS | | ESTABLISH NATIVE PRAIRIE | | ALLOW SUCCESSIONAL |

NORTH AND SOUTH MOUNDS east face

| CROP A ROWS | | ESTABLISH NATIVE PRAIRIE |
| CROP B ROWS | | |

WOODLAND
ON THE MOUNDS

Two to three feet of new soil will be required for cultivation of denser, stratified woodland on the mounds in early stages of the park's development. The new soils would be stabilized and planted with native grassland intially to create a weed-resistant matrix for the gradual interplanting of young tree stock.

Proposed woodland on the mounds is located in areas adjacent to proposed lowland and swamp forests to widen the habitat corridor while conserving the amount of new soil to be imported.

A total of 220 acres of woodland on the mounds is proposed, with 65 acres on the North and South Mounds, and 155 acres on the East and West Mounds.

NORTH AND SOUTH MOUNDS   65 acres

20 A SOIL	ESTABLISH NATIVE PRAIRIE	PLANT
22 A SOIL	ESTABLISH NATIVE PRAIRIE	PLANT
22 A SOIL	ESTABLISH NATIVE PRAIRIE	PLANT

EAST AND WEST MOUND

22 A SOIL	ESTABLISH NATIVE PRAIRIE
22 A SOIL	ESTABLISH NATIVE
22 A SOIL	ESTABL
22 A SO

LOWLAND FOREST

When a supply of native saplings and tree plugs is available (particularly in early years of park construction when other areas are being prepared for planting), lowland and swamp forests are planted in overlapping ecotonal bands on existing soil to build the woodland rim.

EXPRESSWAY CORRIDOR + NORTH AND SOUTH MOUNDS   160 acres

| PLANT | PLANT | PLANT | PLANT | PLANT | PLANT | PLANT |

EAST AND WEST MOUNDS

| PLANT | PLANT |

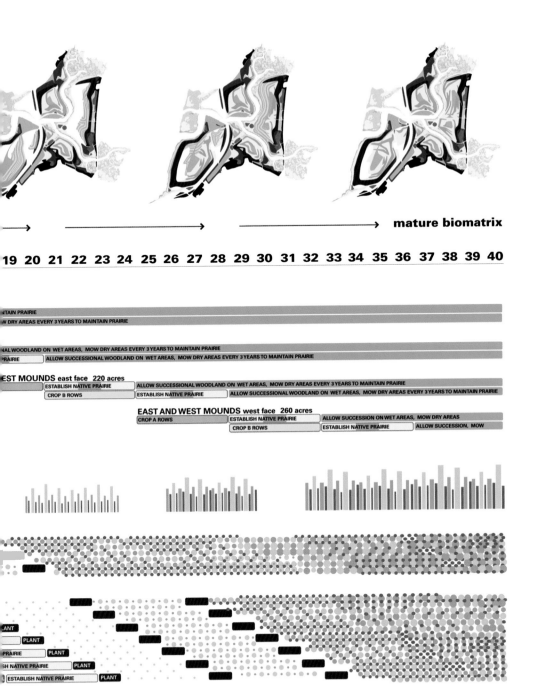

Figure 2 'Ecological transformations for Fresh Kills', Field Operations. © Field Operations.

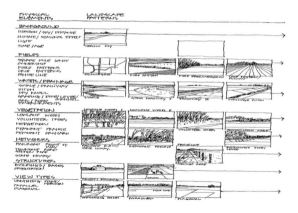

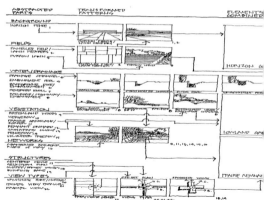

Figure 3 Terry Harkness,'Gardens from Region', 1990. Reproduced by permission of Terry Harkness. © Terry Harkness.

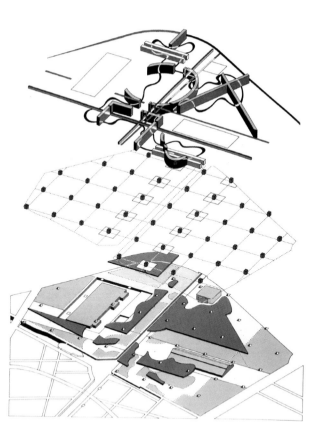

Figure 4 'Points, Lines, Surfaces, Parc de la Villette', Bernard Tschumi Architects, Paris, France, 1982. © Bernard Tschumi.

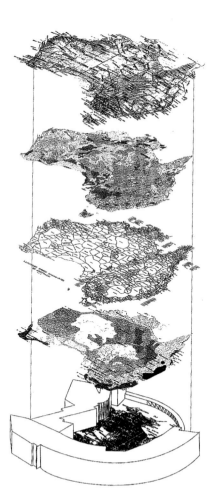

Figure 5 'The Garden of Australian Dreams', Room 4.1.3. Reproduced by permission of Room 4.1.3. © Room 4.1.3.

electoral boundaries, indigenous tribal areas, soils maps and a weather map from Australia Day are assembled in a diagram which is not about formal manoeuvres, as in Tschumi's layers, but has more the sense of a collage, or flatbed[12] compression (figure 5).

As the Gardens from Region diagram illustrates, the distinction between analysis and generative functions is frequently blurred, as retrospective analysis transforms into future possibility. Lawrence Halprin stands out for his use of creative diagramming drawn from music and dance.[13] The 'score'[14] diagrams provide an analytical frame both for existing conditions, as in his 'eco-scores' for the SeaRanch project,[15] and in predicting the future experience of a site, as in his scoring of design permutations.

Indeed, it could be argued that each of these examples in some way subverts any straightforward distinction between analysis and generation functions, in the same way that the simple model of design process as survey–analysis–design[16] has been undermined both by empirical investigation into designers' behaviour[17] and by critique of design creativity[18] and agency.[19] Design diagrams not only simplify and abstract the complexity of the world, both actual and imagined. They also express and articulate the complex nature of design itself.

The Limits of Diagramming the Landscape

Diagrams represent a type of language and, as Wittgenstein remarked, the limits of our language are the limits of our world. For landscape architects, many of the phenomena that are central to practice remain stubbornly beyond the limits of the graphic language, and this in turn constrains both the analytical and the generative potentialities of design. As Burns and Kahn note, 'Graphic tools both inform and bracket how designers think.'[20] Recent theorists such as Corner and Meyer have revealed and highlighted the way that particular choices of design representation shape the outcomes.

Corner[21] notes three particular challenges in representing landscape – its limitless but situated spatiality, the temporality of both experience and medium, and its tactile materiality. We could add a further phenomenological challenge, of expressing the seriality and ephemeral nature of much landscape experience. We also note an epistemological challenge, arising from the paradigmatic shift towards understanding material and human worlds as contingent, evolving, emergent and uncertain 'open' systems.

Landscape's multisensate, spatial and temporal qualities are at the limits of diagramming. Aspects such as the non-visual, the ephemeral and the dynamic do not lend themselves readily to reduction to two or three dimensions. Yet for landscape architecture such attributes are vital, particularly given the current challenges for the discipline. One consequence of the legacy of Picturesque aesthetics in particular, and the general hegemony of visuality at large, is that landscape architecture has found itself in a state of experiential impoverishment, and one challenge of contemporary theory and practice is to overcome this situation.

While designers such as Lynch and Halprin sought to diagram movement through space, the forms of expression remain primarily objective. The phenomenological, felt, experienced landscape, however, is characterised by subjective response, and it is these aspects which exceed the graphic capacity of diagramming. Phenomenological dimensions of the tactile and telluric, the multisensate means of experiencing time and space, and the emotive components of landscape architecture resist representation, let alone the reduction to the spare, two-dimensional frame of a diagram. Smell, for example, cannot even be represented, let alone diagrammed, as the only language of expression we have for the olfactory dimension is text, and even that relies on the language of analogy.

In contrast, the diagrammatic challenge of emergent systems lies not so much in the problem of representing individual subjectivity, but in representing probability. As we indicated in our introductory remarks, landscape architecture has always faced this challenge in actuality – landscape has always been emergent – but earlier generations of designers worked within the security of a more certain, Newtonian world view, in which it was both acceptable and desirable to 'fix' material and action within a conventional and familiar frame of space and time coordinates. Today, such certainties are long gone. However, while digital technologies and computation enable modellers to generate surrogates for emergent landscape processes – through fractal geometries, repeated experiments and multiple scenarios – the essential diagramming problem remains, of how to distil ever increasing degrees of modelling complexity into a graspable whole.

New forms of diagramming and representation are beginning to emerge as reflections of these less tangible and probabilistic factors, including the deployment of montage and unstructured graphic elements such as random blobs or splatters as a means of circumventing precision. Although text has its own limitations it can, arguably, constitute a form of diagram, whether on its own or in combination with graphic elements in the form of an 'image text'. The works of Alan Berger,[22] James Corner,[23] Anuradha Mathur and Dilip Da Cunha[24] explore the use of montage, including images at a range of spatial and temporal scales, and text. Whether or not such representations might be considered diagrams, they attempt to edit and transfigure the complex, ephemeral, uncertain and emergent nature of landscape within abbreviated expressions which are both retrospective and prospective.

Landscape therefore challenges the technology and conventions of architectural diagramming in multiple ways. The biophysical medium itself is in continual flux, and is multiscalar and profoundly complex; the designed experience is ephemeral and transient, while design practice is deeply embedded in social negotiation. As a result, perhaps, the distinguishing feature of landscape architectural diagrams within the wider field of architectural diagramming has been the long-standing emphasis on attempts to capture an essential idea of process. Whether retrospective analysis, prospective imagining, or bridging between the two, landscape architectural diagrams have attempted to convey a sense of dynamic moment – a trajectory or trace. And while modelling technologies enable the creation of ever more complex simulacra, the success or otherwise of diagramming appears to remain with the creative insight of the designers themselves.

Notes
1   RTT Forman, *Land Mosaics: The Ecology of Landscapes and Regions*, MIT Press (Cambridge, MA), 1996.
2   K Olwig, *Landscape, Nature, and the Body Politic*, University of Wisconsin Press (Madison), 2002.
3   J Corner, *Recovering Landscape: Essays in Contemporary Landscape Architecture*, Princeton University Press (New York), 1999.
4   CJ Burns and A Kahn (eds), *Site Matters*, Routledge (New York), 2005.
5   Metaphor literally means to 'carry over', where one thing is used as a substitute for another, and through this to enhance understanding.
6   J Corner, 'Representation and landscape: drawing and making in the landscape medium', *Word & Image*, vol 8 no 3, 1999, pp 243–75.
7   E Meyer, 'Site Citations' in Burns and Kahn, *Site Matters*.
8   I McHarg, 'An Ecological Design Method', *Landscape Architecture*, 1967; I McHarg, *Design with Nature*, Doubleday, (New York), 1969.
9   K Lynch, *The Image of the City*, MIT Press (Cambridge, MA), 1960.
10 D Appleyard, K Lynch and JR Myer, *The View from the Road*, MIT Press (Cambridge, MA), 1965.
11 See Forman, *Land Mosaics*, as an example.
12 'Flatbed' refers to the idea of the printing press, but was used in art by Robert Rauschenberg to express the conception of collage as a surface which collects a range of visual information.
13 L Halprin, 'Motation', *Progressive Architecture*, July 1965, pp 126–33.
14 L Halprin, *The RSVP Cycles: Creative Processes in the Human Environment*, G. Braziller (New York), 1970.
15 L Halprin, *SeaRanch: Diary of an Idea*, Spacemaker Press (Berkeley, CA), 2006.
16 H Sasaki, 'Design Process' in 'Thoughts on Education in Landscape Architecture', *Landscape Architecture*, vol 40 no 4, 1950, pp 158–60.
17 PG Rowe, *Design Thinking*, MIT Press (Cambridge, MA), 1986.
18 SR Krog, 'Is it Art?', *Landscape Architecture*, vol 71 no 3, 1981, pp 373–6.
19 Corner, 'Representation and landscape 1999'.
20 Burns and Kahn, *Site Matters*, p xvii.
21 Corner, 'Representation and landscape, 1999.
22 See for example Alan Berger, *Reclaiming the American West*, Princeton Architectural Press (New York), 2002.
23 See for example J Corner and A Maclean, *Taking Measures across the American Landscape*, Yale University Press (New Haven), 2000.
24 See for example A Mathur and D Da Cunha, *Mississippi Floods: Designing a Shifting Landscape*, Yale University Press (New Haven), 2001.

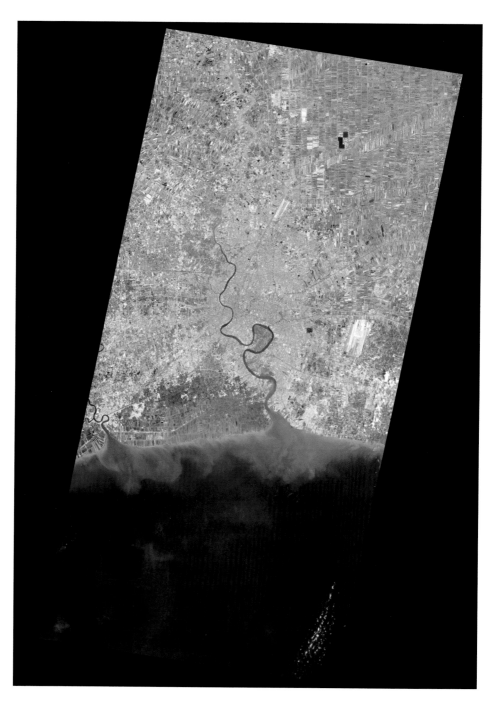

Figure 1 Danaii Thaitakoo, Advanced Spaceborne Thermal Emission and Reflection Radiometer (ASTER) satellite imagery for greater Bangkok. http://asterweb.jpl.nasa.gov/ Infrared. ASTER data is used by Danai Thaitakoo and Brian McGrath at the Chulalongkorn University Landscape Ecology and Planning Lab (Thailand) to obtain detailed maps of land surface temperature, reflectance and elevation in order to develop urban design models for climate change predictions. © Courtesy of Danai Thaitakoo.

Close-up processes of social observation, participant observation and thick ethnographic description can complement the synoptic GIS maps. *Cinemetrics*, a book I co-authored with Jean Gardner, introduces new ways of using digital video in order to develop thick spatial, movement and temporal databases of the relations of urban human and non-human actor networks. *Cinemetrics* describes methods of mining video information to produce diagrams through which space can be generated around social dynamics.[4] With the introduction of digital video, sound and GPS instruments in cell phones, this kind of data-gathering is more and more ready-at-hand and easily distributed (figure 4).

Digital Genealogies: Timeformations
The online interactive website Manhattan Timeformations mixes interactive Flash software with 3-D CAD modelling to create a simple interface in which users can create their own urban diagrams from a database of historical data to discover various events that contributed to the formation of Manhattan's two central business districts.[5] In the digital model that comprises the content of the website, all the high-rise office buildings in Manhattan are positioned both in the geographical space that they occupy and according to their date of construction on a timeline. The z-dimension of this model is time, where 1 year = 30.5 metres (100 feet). This four-dimensional interactive urban diagram can be layered, toggled and repositioned to examine the relationships between spatial and temporal information (figure 5).

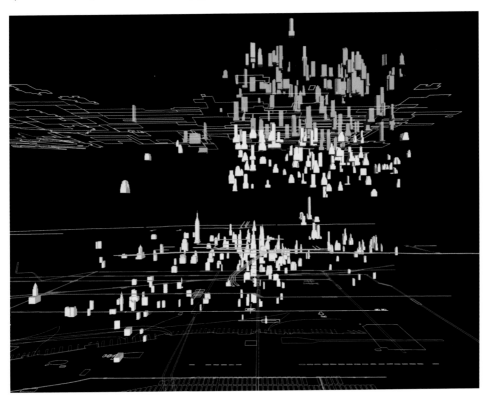

The skyscraper website proved to be very popular with a wide and diverse audience, from schoolchildren to tourists to scientific researchers to digital art organisations. One of the most remarkable partnerships that grew from the work was with the US Forest Service, who recognised that the model created a clear diagrammatic representation of Manhattan's skyscrapers as a social ecology. I was modelling skyscrapers in a way that was similar to how they were modelling forest disturbance and succession. If cities are seen as ecosystems, then time-based Darwinian genealogies studying the descent and emergence of urban form become necessary diagrams for understanding historical processes of urbanisation during a period of rapid urbanisation and climate change.

Patch Dynamics: Ecosystem Feedback Loops

Disturbance ecology is based on the new knowledge that nature operates through the dynamics of constant change and achieves balance or equilibrium only for brief moments in time. Dr Steward Pickett has applied the ecological theory of patch dynamics as a framework to analyse the complex behaviour of urban ecosystems in flux. In the Baltimore Ecosystem Study, directed by Dr Pickett, researchers from over 50 scientific disciplines work with designers on developing new models of urban ecosystem designs. The entire urbanised region of Baltimore is analysed as a dynamic mosaic of land-cover patches draped over a meshwork of intricately drained small watersheds (figure 6).[6] Hydrological monitoring in these small watersheds constantly feeds real-time information to the scientists about the bio-geochemistry of each patch. Designers provide alternative scenarios for these neighbourhood patches whose residents are sampled for their preferences. These preferences are then modelled by the hydrologist to determine the impact of the preferred designs on the water quality, closing a feedback loop between scientific research and design.

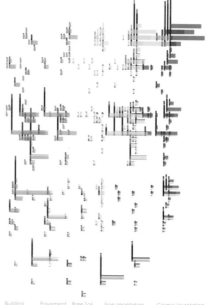

Figure 6 Urban-Interface, Baltimore Patch Signature Chart, 2006. Land-cover signature for the Gwynns Falls Watershed, Greater Baltimore, Maryland. The higher lines indicate the predominance of patches composed of different percentages of building, pavement, bare soil and fine- and coarse-grain vegetated land covers. © Brian McGrath.

Building   Pavement Bare Soil   Fine Vegetation   Coarse Vegetation

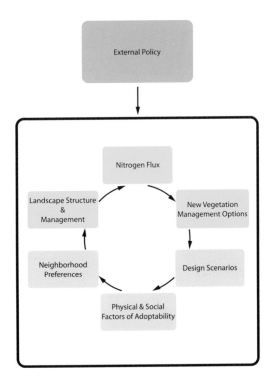

Figure 7 Urban-Interface, Sociecological design feedback loop, 2008. Socioecological design feedback loop, linking nitrogen flux to landscape structure, management and design. Designers are part of a feedback loop between scientists, policy makers, managers and residents, modelling different scenarios which are tested for neighbourhood preference and ecological performance. © Steward Pickett, Mary Cadenasso, Lawrence Band, Jacqueline Carerra, Donald Dennis, Peter Groffman, J Morgan Grove, Brian McGrath and Austin Troy.

Diagrams are used by both scientists and designers throughout such integrated work to help uncover the relationship between the various disciplines, to communicate complex scientific concepts to lay audiences, and to assist people in making design decisions based on performance rather than aesthetics. Diagrams are often the product of collaboration, as they transform from scientific to design concepts throughout feedback loops. In the case of the Baltimore Ecosystem Study, feedbacks loop between ecological monitoring, design modelling, sampling design preferences and modelling the effect of changes (figure 7).

Access and Equity: The Interactive City as Diagram
While GPS, GIS and embedded as well as mobile sensors are the new tools for mapping, monitoring and modelling urban psychosocial natural systems, new methods of diagramming are widely disseminated through text messaging, interactive software and new media and communication technologies. Remote and hand-held sensors are altering the way that we inhabit, imagine and design cities. The character limitations of text messaging has already produced a diagrammatic hieroglyphic language hovering between word and image. The wide dissemination of these tools, symbols and languages through the almost universal distribution of cell phones has tied the vast majority of the world's citizens in a network of noisy feedback loops rather than their being a passive audience of unidirectional broadcast technologies (figure 8).

Figure 8 Urban-Interface, Queens Plaza transit hub, 2002. For Queens Plaza in New York, Urban-Interface designed a luminous floor at the subway platform and overhead screen near the elevated train in order to create an interactive information system which displays transit, weather, traffic, air quality, and security and cultural information, for commuters. © Brian McGrath.

Figure 9 Urban-Interface, Brian McGrath and Jose Echeuvera, Queensborough Bridge bamboo forest, 2002. For the unused space under the Queensborough Bridge, Urban-Interface designed a bamboo grove with a water mister and lighting system tied to air monitoring sensors. Like a monarch butterfly, which increases the colour of its wings by ingesting more milkweed toxins, the mists and lights increase in intensity with the increase in carbon dioxide. © Brian McGrath.

These cell phones are not just communication tools, but are also recording devices with optical lenses and microphones. Soon laser and GPS technology embedded in hand-held devices will make them data-gathering tools as well. Arjun Appadurai has argued for a grass-roots globalisation, where communities are the creators, not the subjects of social science data.[7] Hand-held devices are the important tools in helping these global villagers inhabit, nurture and participate in the design of the forest of symbols that constitutes the contemporary city (figure 9). Will architects be able to expand their roles as symbolic processors to virtual as well as physical environments?

Notes
1   Christopher Small, 'Urban Remote Sensing: Global Comparisons', Brian McGrath and Grahame Shane (eds), *AD Sensing the 21st Century City: Close-up and Remote*, vol 75 no 6, John Wiley & Sons Ltd (Chichester), 2005.
2   Frederic Jameson, *Post Modernism: The Cultural Logic of Late Capitalism*, Duke University Press (Durham, NC); Kevin Lynch, *The Image of the City*, MIT Press (Cambridge, MA), 1960. http://senseable.mit.edu/
3   Bruno Latour, *Reassembling the Social: An Introduction to Actor-Network Theory*, Oxford University Press (Oxford), 2005.
4   Brian McGrath and Jean Gardner, *Cinemetrics Architectural Drawing Today*, Wiley–Academy, a division of John Wiley & Sons Ltd (London), 2007.
5   www.skyscraper.org/timeformations
6   www.beslter.org. This research was supported by funding from the NSF Long-term Ecological Research (LTER) Program.
7   Arjun Appadurai, 'Grassroots Globalization and the Research Imagination', *Public Culture*, vol 12 no 1, 2000, pp 1–19.

Conceptual, minimalist, inclusive, open, collaborative, user-based diagram
(reader/diagrammer can delete as applicable and/or insert their own above)'

Mark Garcia and
(reader/diagrammer can insert name/s here   ).

Begun 2009 completed circa 21st Century/
(reader/diagrammer can insert date of completion here   )

Diagrams and their Future in Urban Design

Peter A Hall

In this new essay on diagrams in urban design, Professor Peter A Hall (University of Texas) traces a theoretical arc of projects and theories that begins, at one pole, with the literally overarching global, top-down, synechdotal, prescriptive, militaristic, idealistic, totalising, aerial, inhuman, viewpoint of the city. This is symbolised by Buckminster Fuller's Geoscope, probably the largest and most ambitious diagram ever imagined. Hall's analysis ends at another pole, with the bottom-up, anecdotal, ground-level, microscopic, individual, partial and experiential views of the city exemplified by the diagrams of (among others) Raoul Bunschoten (CHORA), Atelier Liu Yuyang, James Corner, Natalie Jeremijenko, the Waag Society and Esther Polak, and Damon Rich and CUP. He covers a broad spectrum of work on diagrams in the visualisation of urban knowledge, data and flows, and outlines the strengths and weaknesses, the opportunities and threats, of each. Hall's conclusion on the recent history of the diagram focuses on the criticism that the initial emancipatory, public and non-reductive potential of the diagram has, as yet, not been fully realised and has resulted in little more than iconic, alienating, private, expensive and monumentalising architectures. He proceeds to examine how new technologies and high-tech projects (such as GPRS, GIS, GPS, Google Earth and WikiCity) enable the diagrams that drive a set of innovative, recent design projects, but his focus is also on the economic, anthropological, social, cultural and political impacts of these diagrams. Referencing a broad, multidisciplinary spectrum of theoretical work that includes Claude Lévi-Strauss, Bruno Latour, Guy Debord, Michel de Certeau, Kevin Lynch, Deleuze and Guattari, and Frederic Jameson to support his points, he delineates a series of arguments and problems relating to these new scales and types of urban and high-tech diagrams. He maps out the new experiences of complex and dynamic diagrams of power, globalisation, exploitation, finance, information, people, cities, and their movements and forces, and he cites less well-known examples of practical, collectivist, small-scale, activist projects that use diagrams for catalysing different forms of intelligent, sustainable and environmentally and socially engaged change. He ends this text by moving towards a more futurological, projective position on the post-Deleuzian diagram and, closing his theoretical arc, brings together his contrasting sets of diagrams and theories by finding common ground in the use of the diagram for the reallocation of resources, pushing it to work beyond merely expensive, formalist, private buildings and city spaces. He concludes by calling for the imagination and realisation of diagrams that map and construct a new urban, sustainable and public reality.

Buckminster Fuller's Geoscope, a 61-metre (200-foot) diameter geodesic globe he proposed suspending over the river opposite the United Nations in Manhattan, was the closest the inventor-architect came to designing a kind of energy diagram of the world. Accessed via elevators and underwater tunnel, the Geoscope suggested a kind of public enlightenment by immersion, whereby gazing up at an animated surface graphically representing an inventory of the earth's resources and developmental trends would inspire people, notably architects, to take action. Promoting the scheme in 1961, Fuller told the International Union of Architects in London that it would be the job of architecture schools to study how to render information about the world, and the job of 'architects, inventors and scientists/artists' to accomplish a 'boldly accelerated design evolution' aimed at 'making the world's totally available resources serve 100% of an exploding population'. As Mark Wigley has noted, Fuller's emphasis was on the power of the image, on the imagined revolutionary effect of visualising the earth and its flows: 'Constant observation of these patterns will supposedly enable a more equitable distribution of resources.'[1]

In the last decade, architecture has embraced diagramming as a means to negotiate the complex phenomena of urban design. The diagram has been described as 'mediator between object and subject',[2] as a means of researching and visualising flows – of people, their needs, traffic, goods, weather, construction processes – and as an essential part of the design process. Yet for all its potential, the diagram frequently slips into a familiar role in the architect's rhetorical armoury, fetishised and lending lip service to a process that promised to accommodate stakeholders, yet delivered another monumental structure that alienated them. To imagine a less reductive diagram requires some unpacking of its potency.

Most crucial is an acknowledgment of the situatedness of any diagram, particularly given prevailing myths about the 'truth' of data-gathering and imaging technologies; the way, as Bruno Latour has noted, humans tend to ascribe more truth to machine-made images than to human-made ones.[3] Fuller imagined an image resolution that would allow a viewer to pick out a dot representing his own house inside the Geoscope.[4] But a dot on a map is the very embodiment of insignificance. It is easy to forget that the aerial view is just one perspective, and one with a militaristic genealogy. As Wigley notes, Fuller's embrace of the globe-as-diagram was informed by his personal experience of developing an illuminated globe-data-display system for the situation room of joint chiefs of staff during the Second World War. The aerial view may in fact be better suited to routing, spying and bombing than to urban planning.

The problem is famously articulated in Michel de Certeau's passage written from the top of the World Trade Center in 1984, where he contrasts the top-down view, which 'makes the complexity of the city readable and immobilises its opaque mobility in a transparent text' with the everyday practices of those on the ground, those who 'actually compose the city'.[5] 'These practitioners make use of spaces that cannot be seen; their knowledge of them is as blind as that of lovers in each other's arms ... it is as though the practices organizing a bustling city were characterized by their blindness.' Yet the diagrammatic counterpart to de Certeau's street-level view, the psychogeographic map of a nocturnal wandering composed by Guy Debord and friends from cut-up maps of Paris, has yet to find its way into a city planning meeting. It is one thing to register the subconscious pushes and pulls of a city, to present the city-as-ocean in opposition to the harsh segregation of the Corbusian urbanism being proposed as a solution to slums, but turning that opposition into a planning tool has defied the most ambitious urbanists.

One problem unforeseen by Fuller and his contemporaries was that the comprehensive display of information can overwhelm as well as liberate. As post-war idealism faded, Fuller's overburdened earth-diagram was succeeded by the comprehensive map of networks, of the 'great global multinational and decentered communicational network in which we find ourselves caught as individual subjects', as Fredric Jameson argued in 1988.[6] Jameson called for a cognitive mapping, as a necessary step to make sense of the landscapes of late capitalism, drawing from Kevin Lynch's idea that urban alienation is directly proportionate to the mental unmappability of local cityscapes: 'The incapacity to map socially is as crippling to political experience as the analogous incapacity to map spatially is for urban experience.'[7]

While Jameson's use of an urban metaphor emphasised the importance of lived space and a street-level (or node-level) perspective, the proliferation of maps of the internet that emerged at the turn of the millennium revealed the predominance of the aerial perspective. Barrett Lyon's 2003 'Map of the Internet', a colour-coded array of IP space sprouting outwards in coral-like branches to form an exquisite bauble, served to elicit, primarily, awe. A 2003 Cooperative Association for Internet Data Analysis (CAIDA) map geographically arraying two weeks' activity among 1.2 million IP addresses showed, as Brian Holmes astutely noted, the dominance of the US, Europe and parts of Asia, almost as explicitly as economist Francois Chesnais' 1994 diagram linking the US, Western Europe and Japan in circuits of industrial and financial exchange. But what action might ensue from witnessing a diagram of what Holmes calls the 'near-perfect correlation between the graph of virtual flows and the geography of human exploitation'?[8] He answers by way of the dazzlingly complex power maps of globalisation networks such as 'Influence Networks/World Governance' by activist group Bureau d'etudes (2003): the aim is 'to act as subjective shocks, energy potentials'. Yet as JJ King notes, the Bureau d'etudes maps ultimately show the impossibility of making visible contemporary institutional relationships in a traditional cartographic form.[9] If Fuller's globe-as-data-machine aimed to inspire misplaced hopefulness, viewing these latter-day Geoscopes seems more designed to inspire feelings of powerlessness.

The flurry of artistic projects that followed the Clinton administration's decision to expand civilian use of global positioning systems in 2000 revealed a similar paradox, of the urge to map the flows of people through a city countered by the illegibility of the resulting synoptic diagram. The Waag Society and Esther Polak's spectacular Amsterdam Real Time project of 2002 equipped 60 Amsterdam residents with GPS tracking devices for 40 days; the traces of the residents' movements through the city were transmitted via general packet radio service (GPRS) to a central server which compiled images as sinewy traces on a black screen on display at an exhibition. If the resulting 'live map' of the city as its inhabitants simultaneously created it was compelling, it also served to reinforce the power of the military surveillance technology that relayed it. The aerial view did render the city mobile but it also flattened, decolourised and summarised it. Only the frozen images of individual itineraries, as annotated by their makers, gave a sense of street life, the content of the information on the urban network.

Nevertheless, Amsterdam Real Time was an important precursor for WikiCity, a GIS-based tool for tracking urban street life and traffic flows currently in development at Massachusetts Institutue of Technology's SENSEable City Lab. Described as a planning tool based on actual behaviour, the system was pioneered in Rome in 2007, compiling live city diagrams based on the density of cell phone use patterns (provided by Telecom Italia) and GPS data taken from the positions of city buses. Rome's transportation agency is exploring the use of the resulting data to improve routes and scheduling, while MIT plans to build a wiki-based platform so that citizens and organisations can upload the kind of local information that creates space in the city yet generally remains invisible to satellites: jogging paths, cultural events, environmental conditions and parking spots.

For the human-made wiki-view to become the dominant view requires a conceptual shift. A key tactic is offered by anthropologist Claude Lévi-Strauss: 'To understand a real thing in its totality we always tend to work from its parts. The resistance it offers us is overcome by dividing it.'[10] In design theorist Richard Buchanan's discussion of systems, the shift is seen in phenomenological terms: 'human beings can never see or experience a system, yet we know that our lives are strongly influenced by systems and environments of our own making and by those that nature provides ... We can only experience our personal pathway through a system.'[11] Transferred to the terms of the network, the idea can be rephrased in King's term as 'the node knows – that is knows its own reasons for taking part in the network, with whom it interacts and why, and in what modality'.[12]

Bringing to the foreground the meaning and nature of information moving on a network seems to anticipate new kinds of diagram that explore anecdotal rather than synoptic views. Polak's recent MILK project tracked one movement of the international food trade, in this case, milk produced by Latvian farmers for cheese sold in the Netherlands, 'from the udder of the cow to the plate of the consumer'. The map of the 'MilkLine' is a revealing but relatively small part of a larger mapping project that prioritises narrative accounts of the players involved in this particular flow of resources. Similarly, Polak's 'Nomadic MILK' project, an ongoing project with philosopher of technology Michiel de Lange and cultural anthropologist Ab Drent, aims to trace in a sand painting the GPS-relayed routes taken by nomadic herdsmen and their cattle in Nigeria. One aim of the project is to explore how this mobility, this production of space 'plays a role in the (economic) identities of the participants'.[13]

The significance of the anecdotal, ground-level view to city planning is not as a negotiatory device or a case study 'brought to the table', but what its behaviour tells us about the nature of a self-organising system like a city. In a recently published essay advocating the use of geospatial analysis and technologies in city planning, three researchers – Pietro Pagliardini, Sergio Porta and Nikos Salingaros – characterise the alternative, top-down approach to planning embraced in the 20th century as the prime culprit in bringing about 'inhuman' buildings, 'useless' urban space, and with it the 'failure of an entire discipline'. In place of the separation advocated by Modernist-era planning and the priority it gave to the fastest automotive traffic, Pagliardini et al advocate a strategy they call 'urban seeding'. This would include the use of GIS technology to help enhance our understanding of the 'structural dynamics of change that characterise the evolution of self-organized urban settlements', according to which 'proper policies' can be put in place.[14]

The challenge is in redefining 'proper policy' in terms of the diagram. Pagliardini, Porta and Salingaros align themselves with a prescription for urban morphology closely aligned with the New Urbanist approach – while admitting that is 'unfortunately considered "out of fashion"'.[15] But alongside their case for demolition of the most 'inhuman' structures is a more compelling argument for 'urban seeding' based on 'cheaper interventions on the existing urban fabric'. This seems to pave the way for adaptive reuse, material resourcefulness and the embrace of existing conditions in planning. Again, the diagram, as well as representing existing infrastructure, ground conditions, social and cultural forces, anecdotal views and network behaviour, has potential as a device for constructing a future: a 'real that is yet to come', as Gilles Deleuze and Félix Guattari argue in *A Thousand Plateaus*.[16]

In his seminal essay 'The Agency of Mapping', landscape architect James Corner sets out a number of experimental strategies for a form of urban planning and design that embody the active diagram, concluding with what he called the 'game board' strategy practised by Raoul Bunschoten of the London-based group CHORA. The game board functions as a means of bringing stakeholders to the planning table, writes Corner: 'These are conceived as shared working surfaces upon which various competing constituencies are invited to meet to work out their differences.'[17]

A provocative enactment of this strategy was Damon Rich and the Center for Urban Pedagogy (CUP)'s 1999 'Governor's Island Redevelopment Plan', an exhibition recounting the social processes that accompanied the federal government's recent sale of the East River island to New York State, and the accompanying flurry of proposals for this piece of prime real estate off Manhattan. The centrepiece of the exhibition was a model of the island with movable pieces: visitors were encouraged to make their own proposals for the site.

A further development of the game board idea is currently being explored by CHORA and Shanghai-based Atelier Liu Yuyang Architects, who are part of a consortium pitching to make the Chinese city of Xiamen a 'climate change incubator' using a series of renewable energy and energy efficiency installations funded by the Kyoto Protocol's clean development mechanism (CDM). Traditionally, CDM funding is for large-scale projects such as wind farms, but alternative methods permit the 'bundling' and aggregation of small-scale urban initiatives (such as the distribution of photovoltaic kits in Morocco). Both CHORA's founder Raoul Bunschoten and Liu Yuyang consider it the future work of architects and urbanists to enable and initiate larger development mechanisms rather than respond to pre-established programs. Liu Yuyang characterises the task as something that architects do well: 'realization of a built structure and environment by integrating different needs, desires and constraints'.[18] According to Bunschoten, the projects will be networked with others in the region and tracked in a 'Taiwan Strait Atlas' charting cross-strait renewable energy developments.

Finally, the engineer-artist Natalie Jeremijenko has developed a number of projects that stretch the notion of the diagram as a means to represent traditionally unrepresented stakeholders, be they animal, vegetable or mineral. With OneTrees, Jeremijenko worked with the Bay Area activist group Pond to plant a network of paired, genetically cloned trees that, as they grow, aim to function as 'instruments' registering the social and environmental microclimates of the region.[19] A paper map was produced of the project, but as Jeremijenko argued, 'the whole project is a map – the trees themselves and the way they undergo ongoing growth and change'. A more recent project, OOZ, establishes a network of polycarbonate buoys in the Hudson River that light up when fish are near, encouraging human spectators to feed them food treated with chelating agents that encourage the digestive systems of the fish to cleanse PCBs from their blood. In this instance, as with the Xiamen and OneTrees projects, the map becomes an active network of change, an energy diagram.

Deleuze and Guattari's highly influential concept of the diagram as an 'abstract machine ... a map of relations between forces' has inspired countless interpretations of the concept in architecture, yet which ultimately tend to subordinate the study of relational forces to the generation of intriguing form. On the opposite end of the spectrum, Fuller's Geoscope tended towards the prescriptive, militaristic and idealistic.

The project's structure uses simple architectural and landscape paradigms and shows the reader how these might change in the face of technological change. Elements that are explored in the light of these notions include fountains, dovecotes, vistas, kinetic sculptures, gazebos and temples of repose.

Like any great architecture/landscape project, it has frequent and numerous allusions to the history of art, the history of ideas, the history of architecture and mythology.

Some of the architectural ideas explored include:

- biotechnology, ethics and architecture
- architecture and augmented reality
- remote sensing and the embroidery of space
- networking
- diagramming
- smart materials
- nanotechnology and architecture
- anamorphism and hypertext
- cyborgian architectural geography
- architectural ascalarity
- Herzian space
- mnemonic space
- choreography of chance as a driver for architecture
- cybernetics

I have also tried to identify various types of diagram that might be both analytical and proactive as tools for fuelling the design project. It seems that any useful notational methodology will have to deal with what I have called the '7 Continua of Post-Digital Architecture in the early 21st Century'.

Scratch-Mixing Architecture

The experience of contemporary designers is one of positioning their work in relation to seven continua. These are:

1   Space – there is a continuum of space that stretches from 'treacle' space standing in a field, no computer, no mobile phone, no connectivity whatsoever, to full bodily immersion in cyberspace; along the way between these two extremes are all manner of mixed and augmented spaces.

2   Technology – like space, technology ranges from simple prosthetics (the stone axe) via the Victorian cog and cam, to the valve, capacitor, logic gate, the integrated circuit, the central processing unit, the quantum

computer, the stem cell, the nanobot and a million states and applications between and beyond.

3   Narrative, semiotics and performance – an architect or designer can choose whether their work operates along a continuum that ranges from minimal engagement in quotation or mnemonic nuance in relation to the history of culture or the contemporary world or embraces the multiplicity of the complex and emergent universes of discourse that we inhabit and engage with daily. A design might conjure new conjunctions of semiotics as a way of rereading them. It also might integrate itself with human and cultural memory, and it might be reflexive and performative (in real time or retrospectively).

4   Cyborgian geography – a designer now can posit work which operates in all manner of mixed and augmented terrains that are subject to all manner of geomorphic and cybermorphic factors and drivers.

5   Scopic regimes – architecture can exist at all scales, depending on the resolution of the scope that one chooses to use: continents, oceans, cities, streets, rooms, carpets, microlandscapes and medico-landscape are all part of this continuum.

6   Sensitivity – a designer might decide to make objects, spaces or buildings whose parts are sensitive and pick up environmental variations or receive information. These sensors therefore can make objects and buildings that are influenced by events elsewhere or indeed are influential elsewhere.

7   Time – this is the most important of the continua. All the above six continua can be time-dependent. Therefore designers can 'mix' the movement of their spaces, buildings and objects up and down the other six continua. So a design might oscillate the spaces within itself with varying elements of virtuality over time. A design might use different technologies at different times in its existence. A design might perform complex mnemonic tableaux at certain points in its life cycle. A design might demand of its occupants the use of different lenses with which to see other than anthropocentric phenomena or spaces. A design might coerce the occupant to be aware of environmental conditions in other locations that change. A design might change the sensitivity of objects over time, dulling them sometimes, and making them hypersensitive at other times.

In short, contemporary architecture, like 'non-decorative art, expresses the permanence of objects in substantial physical form, and deals with extended matter in its unchanging aspects: extension, density, duration. These are qualities of an object which are known by analysis and by inference. It is such an object that profound art strives to depict. A work of art of this profound manner is in agreement with all other things of the universe. It has plastic truth.'[2]

Velazquez Machine and Growing Vistas

At the heart of this project are two input machines: the Velazquez Machine, situated in the Orangery in the Tuileries Gardens in Paris, and a not very smart measuring stick placed in and around Bramante's Tempietto in Rome. The stick searches for discrepancies from the idealised and the theoretically repeatable but ultimately unobtainable dimensions of classicism. The Velazquez Machine vibrates to activity on the Web and fish decompose in its centre. All these phenomena are recorded and transmitted back to the mother site in Fordwich and provide the driver data for growing vistas made of aero gel, meandering sculptures and digital chance. The formal quality of this work acts as a memory theatre and quotes from the history of art and virtuality.

To diagram the Communicating Vessels project, I have found it necessary to use various methods of diagramming and these are akin to the drawings of the project themselves. In a project that is fundamentally about the distended cyborgian geographies of the post-digital era, how could they not be?

These diagrammatic typologies are, first, the Psychosemiotic Diagram – a kind of collaged precedent study that brings together some of the nuances and intellectual psychogeography of an element of the project. This is perhaps the simplest of the four and it should be read as a soup of multidimensional associations and aspirations.

Psychosemiotics: A diagram that brings together nuance, reference and aspiration. This one is for a part of the Communicating Vessels project that concerns itself with the archetypal images of the body in art history. © Neil Spiller.

Active Site: This diagram shows the nanodesk base, the small facsimile sculpture that oscillates around the growing vista and the probing of its active site by another element in the project. © Neil Spiller.

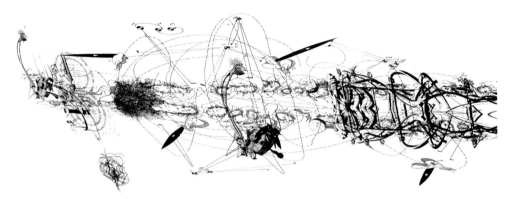

Genesis Mapping: This diagram charts the initial arrangements and dynamics of a particular vista, its start and its end. © Neil Spiller.

The second diagram is called 'Genesis Mapping' and concerns itself with the initial structure of a system, in effect the architecture before the architecture, the systematics before the algorithms of change start acting, reconfiguring. It talks about the progression of objects and space along one of the vistas, and charts the dynamics and geometries and their points of view and transition.

The third notation is one that concerns itself with the dynamics of chance that reconfigure space and is called the 'Active Site' diagram. It concerns itself with the time-based opportunities of change and the possibilities of rewiring previously wired and expedient input and output drivers. So, for example, at a certain point in time the dynamics of a moving sculpture moving around a growing vista instead of being conditioned by a vibrating plumb line in Paris might be influenced by something else within the project. It is also imagined that small nanotech facsimiles of the main project will reside on a nanotech desk (mixing desk) and over time continually remix themselves in a sexual manner to rewire the whole scheme.

Individual surfaces or elements become more or less sensitive over time, and this aspect of the project is represented by 'Homunculitic Diagrams'. I illustrate this with a group of homunculitic drawings that portray the sensitivity of the bread element with the 'Dalinian Leg' sensor that is sited in an arrow slit in the Dali Museum in Spain and collects data that informs a vista's progress and growth.

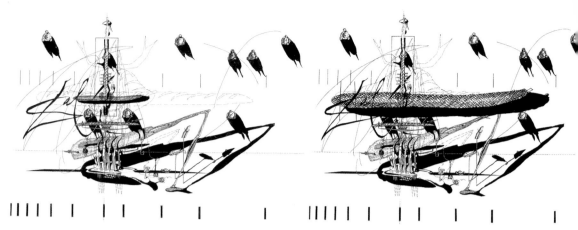

Homunculitic: This series of three diagrams shows the increase in surface sensitivity of the sculptural bread motif over time. © Neil Spiller.

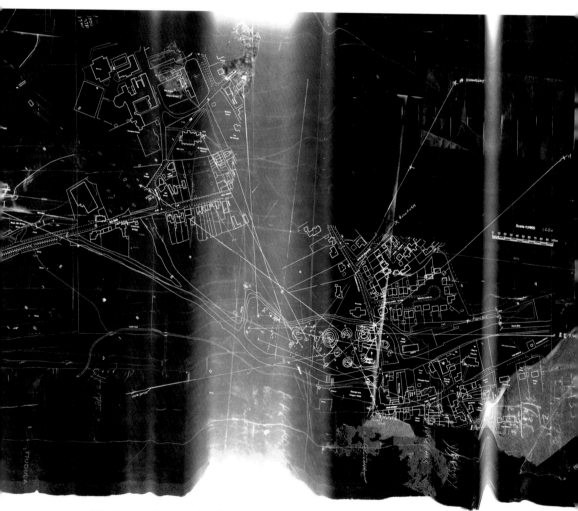

This drawing shows the location of the Communicating Vessels island in Fordwich, Kent, UK and vista positions. © Neil Spiller.

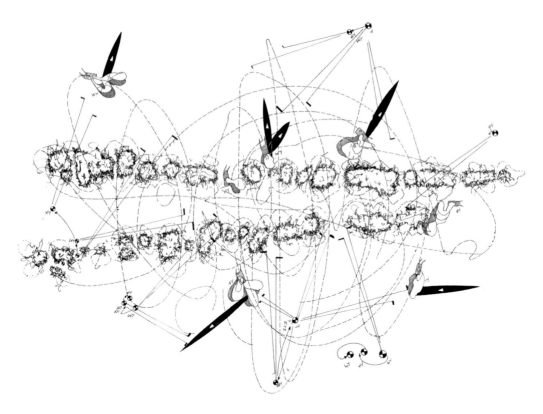

A particular vista and its time-based dynamics. © Neil Spiller.

We know that as the 21st century dawns we are capable of making exceptional architectures that immerse themselves in their peculiarities. These conditions can be intensely ecological, systematically open-ended, driven by imperatives of chance, glocal, intellectually founded, enabling, concerned with time and duration, synthetic with natural landscapes, using computational power not just as a means of representation but as an editing spatial engine, and we can create reflexive architecture that can embroider space with swift and changing exquisite cybernetic chunkings.

Above all, we need to develop ways to understand and develop these new architectural dynamics. I believe the Communicating Vessels project with its diagramming strategies is a step in the right direction.

Notes

1 Charles E Gauss, *The Aesthetic Theories of French Artists*, The John Hopkins University Press (Baltimore, MD), 1949, p 85.
2 Gauss, *The Aesthetic Theories of French Artists*, p 71.

Part III: Diagrams

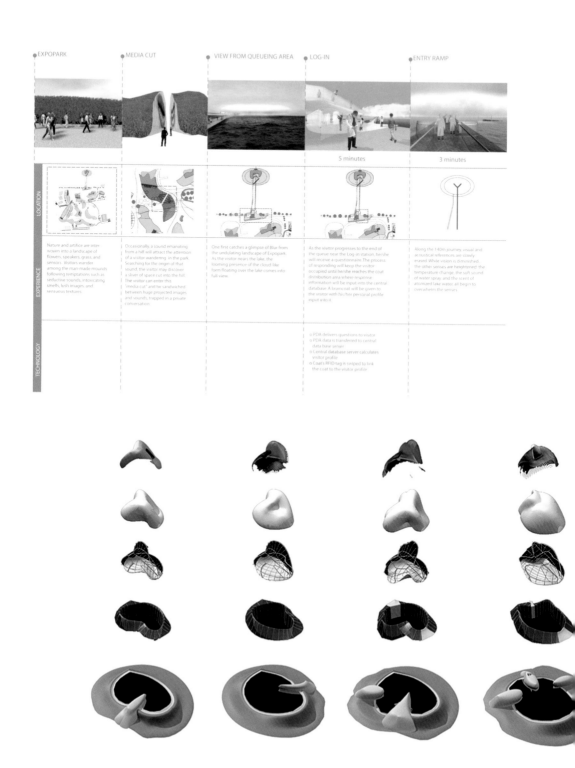

EXPOPARK · MEDIA CUT · VIEW FROM QUEUEING AREA · LOG-IN · ENTRY RAMP

5 minutes · 3 minutes

LOCATION

EXPERIENCE

Nature and artifice are interwoven into a landscape of flowers, speakers, grass, and sensors. Visitors wander among the man-made mounds following temptation such as seductive sounds, intoxicating smells, lush images, and sensuous textures.

Occasionally, a sound emanating from a hill will attract the attention of a visitor wandering in the park. Searching for the origin of that sound, the visitor may discover a sliver of space cut into the hill. The visitor can enter this "media cut" and be sandwiched between huge projected images and sounds, trapped in a private conversation.

One first catches a glimpse of Blur from the undulating landscape of Expopark. As the visitor nears the lake, the looming presence of the cloud-like form floating over the lake comes into full view.

As the visitor progresses to the end of the queue near the Log-in station, he/she will receive a questionnaire. The process of responding will keep the visitor occupied until he/she reaches the coat distribution area where response information will be input into the central database. A braincoat will be given to the visitor with his/her personal profile input into it.

Along the 140m journey, visual and acoustical references are slowly erased. While vision is diminished, the other senses are heightened: the temperature change, the soft sound of water spray and the scent of atomized lake water, all begin to overwhelm the senses.

TECHNOLOGY

□ PDA delivers questions to visitor.
□ PDA data is transferred to central database server.
□ Central database server calculates visitor profile.
□ Coat's RFID tag is swiped to link the coat to the visitor profile.

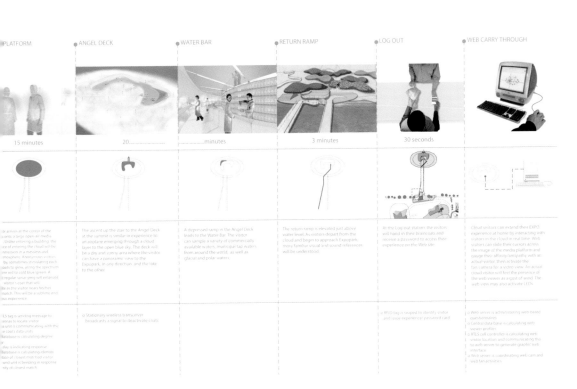

PLATFORM	ANGEL DECK	WATER BAR	RETURN RAMP	LOG OUT	WEB CARRY THROUGH
15 minutes	20........................minutes		3 minutes	30 seconds	

above: Storyboard diagrams of the Blur and Braincoat projects for the Swiss Expo, Neuchatel, Switzerland, 2002. The diagram as narrative organisational system for an architectural project is here used as a storyboard to integrate and interrelate representational drawings and 'Technology', 'Experience' and 'Location' across time in this dynamic, interactive and intelligent architecture. © Courtesy of Diller, Scofidio + Renfro.

left: Diagrams sequence of the Embryological House©™, 1998. The Embryological House can be described as a strategy for the invention of domestic space that engages contemporary issues of brand identity and variation, customisation and continuity, flexible manufacturing and assembly. Identified by a system of geometrical limits that allows for endless variations and the possibility for novelty and recognition, this design marks a shift from a Modernist mechanical kit-of-parts design and construction technique to a more vital, evolving, biological model of embryological design and construction. Designed using animation software, the Embryological House is a 4-D diagram. © Greg Lynn FORM.

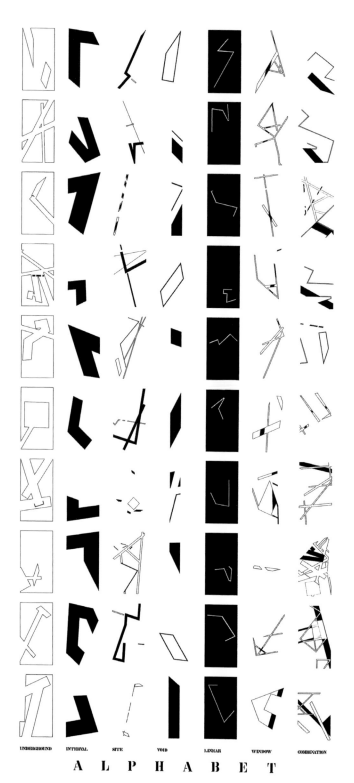

UNDERGROUND   INTERNAL   SITE   VOID   LINEAR   WINDOW   COMBINATION

A L P H A B E T

Between the Lines,
Architectural Alphabet,
Jewish Museum, Berlin,
1988–9. A diagram of an
alphabet of architectural
diagrams. Reproduced by
permission of Studio
Daniel Libeskind.
© Studio Daniel Libeskind.

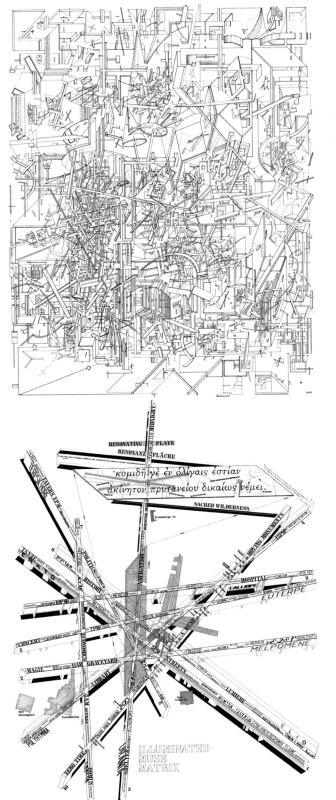

Maldoror's Equation, Micromegas, 1979. A congested, Constructivist maelstrom and agglomeration of uncertainly interrelated but ascalar and seemingly individually meaningless diagrams. The diagrams exist as notations between architectural symbols, components, details, geometric and platonic solids and their projected derivatives. These interpenetrating diagrams exist in a chaotic, illusory and contradictory multitude of different spaces which disrupt and deconstruct each other. The virtual, idealising and tumultuous qualities of these works were to influence the diagrammatic work of later digital architects such as Marcos Novak and whole schools of architecture. Reproduced by permission of Studio Daniel Libeskind. © Studio Daniel Libeskind.

Out of Line, Illuminated Muse Matrix, Urban Competition, Postdamer Platz, Berlin, 1991. Note the unprecedented integration of text and diagram. Reproduced by permission of Studio Daniel Libeskind. © Studio Daniel Libeskind.

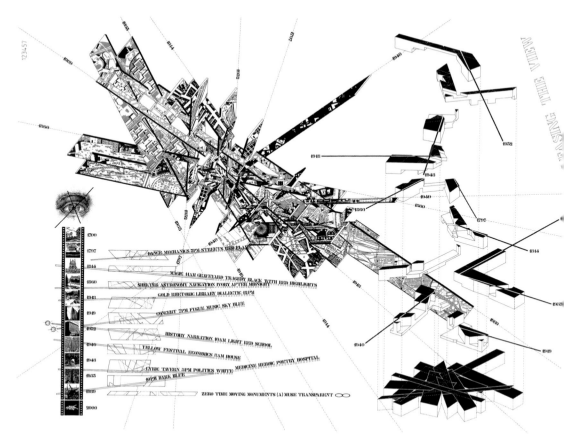

Out of Line, Conceptual Diagram, Urban Competition, Postdamer Platz, Berlin, 1991. The identity of text and diagram is evolved and articulated (in the context of a chronological analysis of Potsdamer Platz) into 3-D historical narratives and within urban diagrams extrapolated into the future of Berlin. Reproduced by permission of Studio Daniel Libeskind. © Studio Daniel Libeskind.

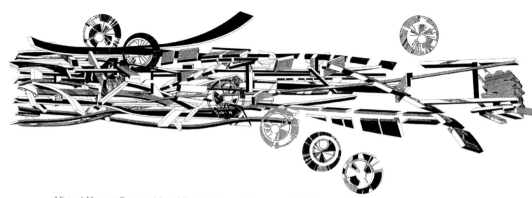

Virtual House Competition, Virtual House Diagram, 1997. Reproduced by permission of Studio Daniel Libeskind. © Studio Daniel Libeskind.

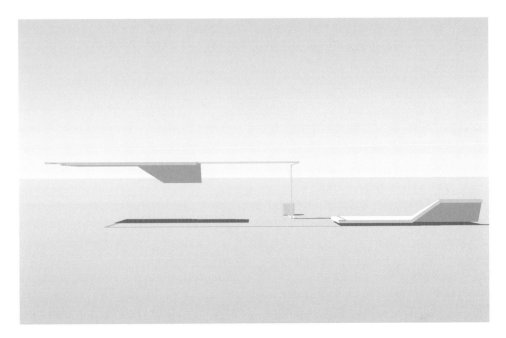

3-D Diagram of Physical Structure, Digestible Gulfstream, 2008. Deliberately functional, abstract and minimal, this diagram of the physical structure represents the infrastructure for an invisible architecture of air. © Philippe Rahm architectes/Piero Macola.

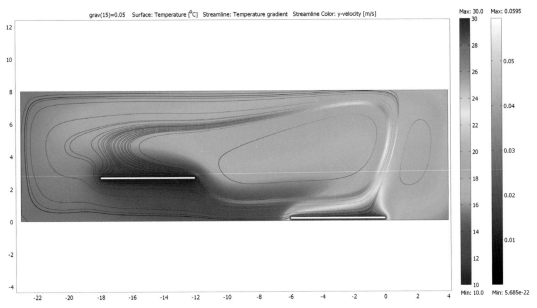

Diagram of Temperature and Air Velocity, 'Digestible Gulfstream', Venice Biennale, 2008. 'Digestible Gulf Stream' is the prototype for architecture that works between the neurological and the atmospheric, developing like a landscape. The diagram of air temperature, and velocity gradients and fields of the space, give the design for this architecture. © Philippe Rahm architectes/Piero Macola.

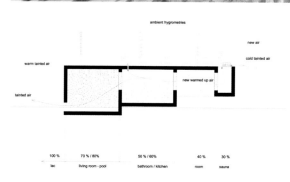

above and left: Philippe Rahm, Mollier Houses, Vassivière, Limousin, France, 2005. Based on a Mollier diagram (thermodynamic diagram of temperature and humidity of air) this holiday house design is unusual in that Mollier diagrams are normally used for the design work associated with energy plants (including nuclear), compressors, steam turbines, refrigeration systems, and air-conditioning and ventilation systems to spatialise the cycles of thermodynamic systems. © Philippe Rahm architectes.

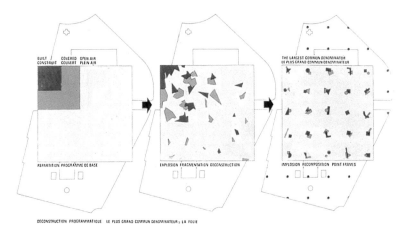

Bernard Tschumi Architects, built/covered/open,
Parc de la Villette, Paris, 1982. © Bernard Tschumi.

For Tschumi, the future of the diagram in architecture, what there is still left for the diagram to achieve in architecture, is clear:

In terms of my present and future work on the diagram, I am not interested in the diagram as a short cut towards an icon. I am also fascinated by the idea of having to diagram something in the small, on a postage stamp. If I don't have much room to express many ideas, I have to concentrate, to edit the most important part of what I want to say. Imagine asking a novelist, 'Write the main ideas of your book on a postage stamp.' The *reductio ad absurdum* is enormously important in the history of architecture. Whether it is in the dimension of time, or in the double colonnade of the Louvre, San Pietro in the Vatican or the Villa Savoye, or the Farnsworth House, every time it is a cartoon but it still contains a concept, a certain moment in the history of architecture and the ways people looked at architecture. So because there is no architecture without concept, the diagram can become central to my discovery of new concepts, three- and four-dimensional, architectural concepts. If you had asked me, 'Precisely what kinds of concepts and diagrams?', say 20 to 25 years ago, I would have responded, 'Programme.' Programme is a thing that one needed to explore. Now I feel reasonably comfortable about understanding how it works. If you had asked me the question 15 years ago, I would have said, 'Vectors and envelopes.' Five years ago, I would have said, 'The information and the combination between concept, content and context.' At the moment I am working on very long-term, large-scale projects. So my interest again is very much about exploring, at the city scale, those same issues. But now I have to deal with utilities, infrastructure, financial flows and all of that. You need to conceptualise this because these are not forms, they are very abstract and complex. The definition of the word 'city' may have to do with 'a substantial amount of noise'. These days, reducing the level of pollution, traffic and the level of noise is totally against the idea of cities.

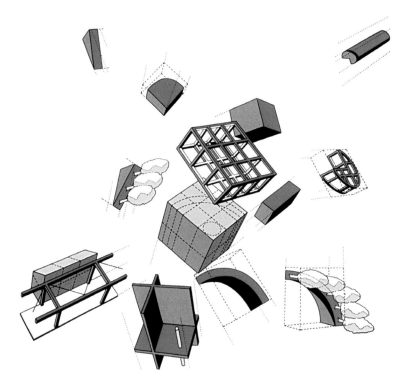

Bernard Tschumi Architects, exploded *folie*, Parc de
la Villette, Paris, 1982. © Bernard Tschumi.

The city has always been the place of congestion and always been the place
where it was noisier; it was always the place that was more polluted; it used to
stink of shit and piss. The point is that the inherent purity of architecture is
always there and tries to reduce those dimensions.

Describing the subject of the future of the diagram and new technologies, of diagrams in
softwares, interfaces and in their parametric and interactive forms, Tschumi concludes that:

For me the diagram is a device, a tool that I am always using, that I am improving,
that is an extension of my mind. Whether that tool is used with digital techniques
or as a scribble, that is still just the graphic extension of my brain. New
technologies are very important and not just in architecture. New technologies
and visualisations can completely change, not only what a city looks like but the
way it works, land values, the economy, lifestyle, everything. But the inventor of
the light bulb or of electricity also completely changed it all. These are things
that happen in the realm of architecture which are part of an overall, wider
research project. However, I can't see the diagram disappearing, as it is a
mediation and you need to go through that mediation. But architecture is also
about sensation, physicality, experience. For example, the Gothic cathedral is

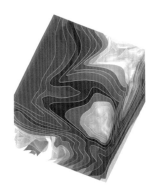
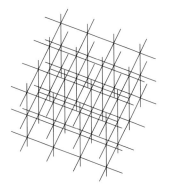

Atlas of Novel Tectonics
Reiser + Umemoto

Machinic Phylum

[M]aterial behaviour takes an active role in the genesis of new structural forms. Moreover, the forces that act on the component model behave diagrammatically, in that they can be rescaled to those of an entire tower.[1] Like the relationship between intensive and extensive logics, or the relationship between matter force logics and codification systems, architects are inevitably implicated in the tension between the generative and limiting poles of both. The potentials that flow off of this tension inevitably find their expression within multiple levels, from the non-human stuff of construction to the character of a building's occupation. This burgeoning machinic reservoir is tapped through the agency of the diagram.

The Diagram

Material organisations at the macroscale must of necessity be modelled in order to predict or track changes to their behaviour. Thus an analogue connection must be made to microscale. Macro-organisations of material behaviour can be approximated at smaller scales, but adjustments are necessary as the system becomes rendered in a more intensive or more extensive model. For instance, a model aeroplane cannot be exactly scaled down and expected to operate in flight, because the behaviour of airflow and lift is not consistent at the smaller scale. For this reason, operable model aeroplanes must undergo deformation in the wing according to a coefficient of scale dictated by a dimensionless parameter known as the Reynold's number. A 1960s-era model of a water table approximated by networks of resistors and transistors is an example of an analogue model at a small scale of larger scale properties. First pump tests at square mile intervals calculate average values of capacity and flow for the water table. These values are represented by resistors and transistors in an electrical field. The behaviour of material at one scale allows scientists to predict its behaviour at another. The implications of this scalability of material behaviours has far-reaching implications for architecture.

The medium of these implications is the diagram, which provides an abstract model of materiality. Such a diagram can be derived from any dynamic system at any scale. A close tracking of a certain dynamic (temperature, pressure, wind speed, etc) can be mapped as a gradient field that can be abstracted from its origins or its material source. A diagram of

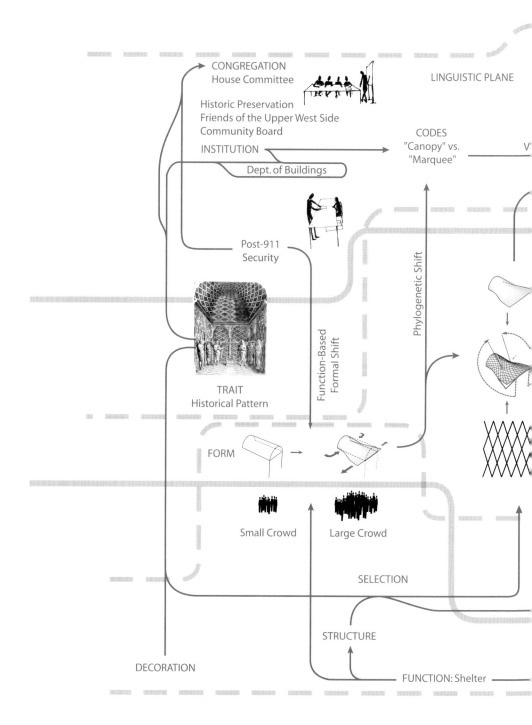

CONGREGATION
House Committee

LINGUISTIC PLANE

Historic Preservation
Friends of the Upper West Side
Community Board

INSTITUTION

CODES
"Canopy" vs.
"Marquee"

V

Dept. of Buildings

Post-911
Security

Phylogenetic Shift

Function-Based
Formal Shift

TRAIT
Historical Pattern

FORM

Small Crowd   Large Crowd

SELECTION

STRUCTURE

DECORATION

FUNCTION: Shelter

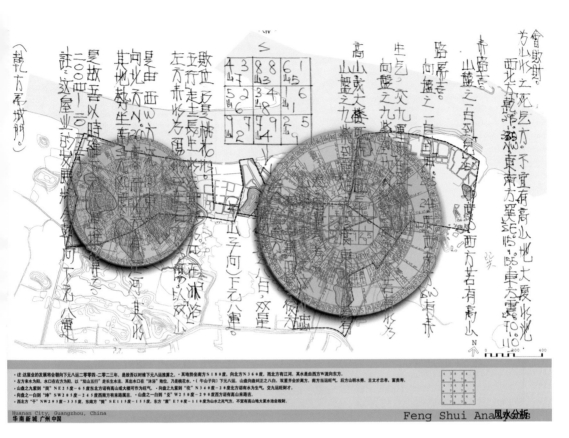

Ken Yeang, Feng Shui Diagram, Hunan City, Guangzhou, China, 2008. Feng shui analysis diagram for the urban design of the city. © TR Hamzah and Yeang, Sdn. Bhd. 2008.

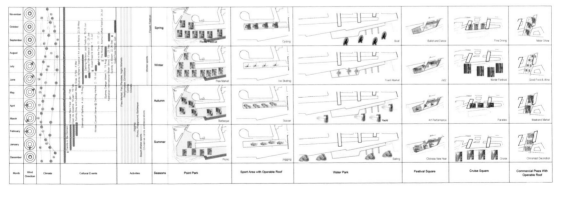

Ken Yeang, Green Square, Sydney, 2008. Programming diagram analysing seasonal factors in the spatial design for multiseasonal cultural activities and events in an urban public space. © TR Hamzah and Yeang, Sdn. Bhd. 2008.

Architectural Evolution
The Pulsations of Time

Charles Jencks

Architect and theorist Charles Jencks's 'Structural diagram or semantic space for 20th-century architecture' was the first diagram of the evolution of 20th-century architecture and is (along with its later incarnations) one of the most critical, rigorous and exhaustive diagrams of theory and practice in the history of architecture. In this newly commissioned essay on the uses of diagrams to map the history and future of architecture, Jencks contextualises, and reflects on his 35 year long diagrammatic contributions to the emerging field of architectural evolution. Drawing on biological evolutionary theory, semiotics and the philosophy of history in Darwin, Haeckel, Kubler and Stephen Jay Gould, he demonstrates the erasures, errors, prejudices and biases implicit in similar kinds of taxonomic, phylogenetic and genealogical diagrams and diagrammatic practices and texts. In its tracing of the lineage of evolutionary diagrams, Jencks's visual analysis makes links to Egyptian king lists, biblical family trees, Banister Fletcher's The Tree of Architecture, Alfred Barr's canonical diagram of Modern Art/Cubism and Abstract Art and Charles Osgood's 3-D semiotics diagrams. Jencks argues for the diagram's value as an interpretative, historical and theory-building tool and an object/product of knowledge, as well as a generative, projective, predictive and futurological methodology. Jencks's conclusions on the possible problems and possibilities inherent in the diagramming of architecture suggest higher-level research projects and an emerging subdiscipline with perhaps an even more digitally driven generative, diagrammatic future for architectural evolution.

It is a truism to say architecture evolves, and almost equally obvious to add that there are compelling social consequences of evolution. Those who know where it will go next will, like market traders, stay ahead of the game. Is it a surprise that Deyan Sujdic titled the 2002 architectural biennale in Venice NEXT, or that this was also the name of a popular fashion chain in the 1990s (now less fashionable)? Pre-empting the Zeitgeist is not only a question of keeping up with the Joneses; in the Darwinian economy, it is an important part of any architect's survival. It is thus another truism to say architects compete for scarce jobs in a shifting social economy, and finding out where that will move next creates a number one anxiety in any large office, even for those who go counter to the trends. It pays to know how to be different in just the right way, like the investor and contrarian Warren Buffet or the office of Frank Gehry. Just as Adam Smith's hidden hand selects out inefficient producers, just as Darwin's natural selection drives some species to extinction, so the building Zeitgeist can be a Grim Reaper.[1]

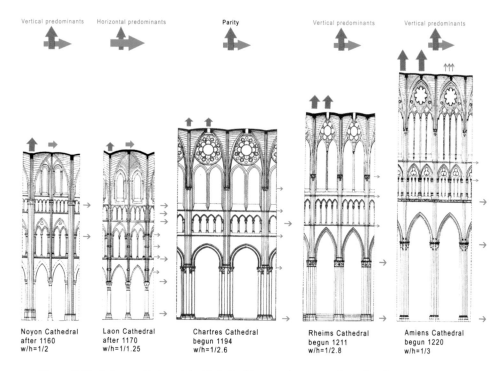

Figure 6 Evolutionary Series of the High Gothic over sixty years, based on Pevsner and Panofsky. Horizontal architectonics in green, vertical in red, and summary at the top. General trends towards height and slenderness ratios are more clear than the impact of details and refinements, for instance the red lines in the Rheims triforium. But, as Panofksy shows, these were noted by contemporary architects. Chartres' nave is often seen as the classic balance between the two visual forces though Panofsky sees it as 'horizontal supremacy.' © Charles Jencks.

bipartite plate-tracery window, the triforium still … consists of perfectly equal interstices separated by perfectly equal colonnettes; horizontal continuity rules supreme all the more so because the string courses overlap the wall shafts. (p 76)

'Horizontal continuity rules supreme' − it is as easy to criticise such *obiter dicta* as it is Haeckel's Man. However, the point is *not* whether Chartres' nave elevation shows Pevsner's 'vehement' balance or rather Panofsky's 'horizontal supremacy', but the way their analyses illuminate evolution, and choices the architects have made.

Viewed through the eyes of a biologist, the diagram shows an aesthetic and technical beauty emerging over time, from several forces (figure 6). One can follow the way the small triforium level emerges at Noyon above the gallery level to create a horizontal movement and lighten the wall surface in front of the pitched roof (that one doesn't see), then follow how, at Laon, all the little horizontal annulets around the shafts, and the string courses, further the horizontal emphasis. And then the way Chartres drops the gallery level and unifies the quadripartite bay in the classic solution, and the way Rheims and Amiens increase the height, squeeze the proportions vertically, add subtle accents to

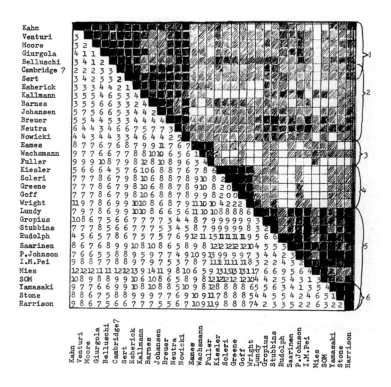

Figure 10 American architects – the relationships between, as determined by numerical taxonomy, 1972. Here the six major schools can be seen by the darker shading (or numbers): from the top, the Academic, Environmental, Technical, Organic, Formalist, and Pragmatic. See *Architectural Design*, November 1969, p. 582, for a further discussion. © Charles Jencks.

As I was working on these evolutionary trees, classification in biology was becoming ever more sophisticated owing to genetic research and the computer. This forced me to consider evolutionary relationships more closely. For my thesis, written under Reyner Banham, had a chapter on recent American architecture where devilish pluralism threatened to obliterate all diagrams. It was too complex and subtle to capture in an evolutionary tree. So, surveying the riotous field of 34 leading architects, I applied the recent method from biology – numerical taxonomy – and came up with a new diagram of relatedness.[8] It used 12 different taxons, or identifiers, and computing these by hand resulted in a grid of numbers and shades of grey (figure 10). These bring out the strong and weak clusters, again attractor basins which I saw as varying from more 'academic' architects at the top to the 'pragmatic' and commercial ones on the bottom. But this method was partly a blind alley, as well. Although it helped to illuminate the subtlety of variation, it was more than a historian needed to portray. Who, except some rarefied archibotanist, cares about so many shades of grey? The lesson was clear.

Diagrams of history must simplify to tell various stories, and their complexity must mimic the pulsations of time, but their organisation must also reflect more than the historian's bias.

space, he said, and lay out the crisscrossing themes on tables and walk among them. Better today to lay them out in hyperspace and fly among them on the computer, rearranging with other historians the clusters of architects as they too navigate their field (figure 13). One can well imagine a collective research project, funded by a university and aided by the Web, which makes architectural history a more accurate reflection of architectural evolution. One anticipates this *nuova scienta* with pleasure.

Notes

1 The economic theory of Adam Smith and his hidden hand that magically selects marketable commodities led directly to Charles Darwin's theory of natural selection. These twin pillars of Modernism led many people to confuse such forces with the Zeitgeist, the spirit of the age. Karl Popper and others have rightly attacked the confusion and the way the Nazis among others, including the Modernists, used the Zeitgeist to stampede an audience towards their movements. Ironically Warren Buffet, the second richest man in the world, made his fortune as the economic contrarian – going against the Zeitgeist. Of course, there are fashions and climates of opinion, and traditions that look like a Zeitgeist, and curators title their shows The Zeitgeist to amplify the stampede, a typical abuse of history.

2 George Kubler, *The Shape of Time: Remarks on the History of Things*, Yale University Press (New Haven), 1962, pp 33–9, 53–61.

3 Nikolaus Pevsner, A*n Outline of European Architecture* [1943], Penguin Books (Harmondsworth), 7th edn, 1963, pp 97–110, p 107; Erwin Panofsky, *Gothic Architecture and Scholasticism* [1951], Meridien Books (Cleveland, Ohio), 1957, 9th printing, 1968, pp 74–88, p 76. Such formal analysis may look arcane, but many German and American scholars of the same generation debated whether the curtain walls of Modernists such as Louis Sullivan were, basically, horizontal or vertical. Giedion, in *Space, Time and Architecture*, Harvard University Press (Cambridge, MA), 1967, p 392, caption) decides these Chicago windows are both, and thus the 'neutrality' of the Chicago frame is confirmed. It follows for subsequent historians, for Colin Rowe, that Le Corbusier's diagram of the Chicago frame is seminal. It becomes the Doric column of Modernism, an idea that comes from a close reading of formal change.

4 Kenneth Frampton, *The Evolution of 20th Century Architecture: A Synoptic Account*, SpringerWienNew York, China Architecture & Building Press, 2007.

5 Charles Jencks and George Baird (eds), 'History as Myth', in Meaning in Architecture, George Braziller (London and New York), 1969, pp 245–65; at the behest of Reyner Banham first published in Bartlett Transactions, London, in 1968.

6 William Richards, 'Architecture or Evolution: Charles Jencks' Evolutionary Tree', A Thesis presented to the Faculty … School of Architecture, University of Virginia, 2006.

7 Richards, 'Architecture or Evolution', for references The next use of Osgood's semantic space was in *Architecture 2000: Predictions and Method*, International Thomson Publishing (New York and London), 1971, p 40, re-edited as *Architecture 2000 and Beyond*, Wiley-Academy (London), 2000, also p 40. The notion of attractor basins becomes well defined in complexity theory during the 1990s.

8 This diagram is the basis for chapter 6 of my *Modern Movements in Architecture*, Penguin Books (Harmondsworth and New York), 1973, and subsequent editions, p 188.

9 This diagram is discussed in many contexts but most completely in Charles Jencks, 'Canons in Cross Fire: On the Importance of Critical Modernism', *Harvard Design Magazine*, Cambridge, MA, 2001, and reprinted in William S Saunders (ed), *Judging Architectural Value*, University of Minnesota Press (Minneapolis), 2007, pp 52–65; and *Critical Modernism: Where is Postmodernism Going?*, Wiley-Academy (London and New York), 2007, pp 203–18.

Martha Markopoulou, Soft oscilating device. From *The Missing Equipment of the Barbarians*, 2006. A diagram based on the translation of the novel *Salammbô*, by Gustave Flaubert, into a series of softly oscillating devices that translate the conditions of the narrative of the novel into architectural spaces. © Martha Markopoulou.

The increasing speed of change and complexity of the planet, its cities and the kinds of activity humanity is more and more engaging in, will create new kinds of qualitatively and quantitatively different problems. These will become bigger and more complex, requiring new kinds of global, multidisciplinary systems of innovation and design. But they will need to be solved by a combination of an overall view and ever increasing levels of precision and control at decreasing levels of size. Smallness is becoming the key to resolving the problems of bigness. Architectural and urban problems will require integration and engagement with larger regional and global, more long-term and long-range problems and conditions, and 'spime'-like, distributed, immaterial, invisible systems of experience and service design.[7] Designed interventions will (in some cases) operate at, and require design and implementation at, nano-, pico-, femto- and microscales, mediated, monitored and controlled through diagrams (as opposed to the more traditional, visible, object-building and perceivable interventions of previous centuries).

As the different dimensions, scales, qualities, intensities and types of space increase their effects on each other and become increasingly designed, new levels and types of multiscalar, complex, integrated spatial design will be created. These will use and generate transfers of diagrams research between formerly unconnected domains. As a more integrated kind of research diagrams, this growing body of knowledge will acquire the status, structure and identity of a more coherent discipline and domain in its own right. And as the importance of the design of diagrams to knowledge-building is increasingly recognised, the importance of architects and spatial designers as skilled makers of highly extensible diagrams will also increase. As a result, academic departments, research centres, courses, organisations, institutions, consultancies and offices that specialise in diagrams and their design will emerge to exploit this new global opportunity and market.

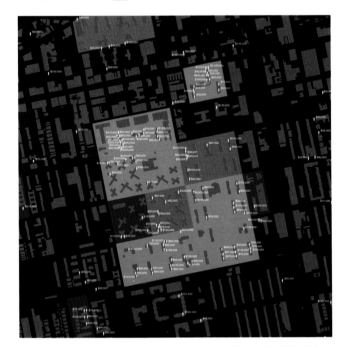

BROOKLYN,
NEW YORK CITY

ADDED UP BLOCK BY BLOCK, IT COST
$359 MILLION DOLLARS TO IMPRISON
PEOPLE FROM BROOKLYN IN 2003,
FACILITATING A MASS MIGRATION
TO PRISONS IN UPSTATE NEW YORK.
95% EVENTUALLY RETURN HOME.

Architecture and Justice, 2006.
From the Million Dollar Block
project, Spatial Information
Design Lab, GSAPP, Columbia
University. Migration diagram,
showing mass migrations from
Brooklyn to upstate prisons.

Million Dollar Block Project,
Spatial Information Design
Lab, GSAPP, Columbia
University. People Dollars
diagram, Architecture and
Justice, 2006. Using GIS
software, this diagram shows
the costs of criminalising and
incarcerating residents of
New York City blocks.

Images top and left courtesy
of Architecture and Justice
2006, Spatial Information
Design Lab, GSAPP,
Columbia University, Project
Team: Laura Kurgan (project
director) Eric Cadora, David
Reinfurt, Sarah Williams.

BROWNSVILLE,
BROOKLYN

IT COST 17 MILLION DOLLARS TO IMPRISON
109 PEOPLE FROM THESE 17 BLOCKS
IN 2003. WE CALL THESE MILLION DOLLAR
BLOCKS. ON A FINANCIAL SCALE
PRISONS ARE BECOMING THE
PREDOMINANT GOVERNING INSTITUTION
IN THE NEIGHBORHOOD.

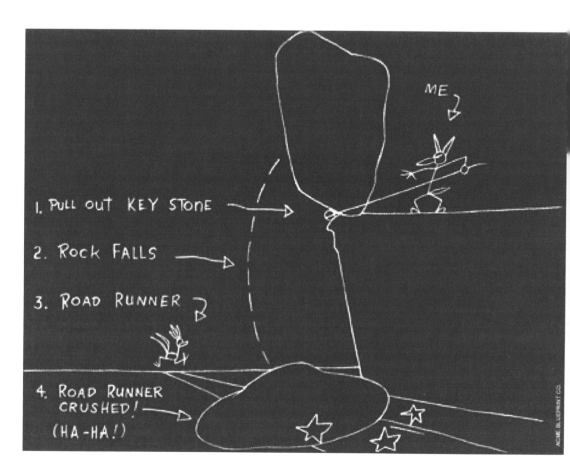

Blueprint Diagram by Wiley Coyote, 2008.
Diagram for the 'Road Runner' cartoon, inspired
by Chuck Jones. Courtesy Chuck Jones Centre
for Creativity. © Linda Jones Enterprises.

Select Bibliography

Abrams, J and P Hall (eds), *Else/Where: Mapping New Cartographies of Networks and Territories*, University of Minnesotta Design Institute (Minneapolis, MN), 2006

Andersen, M, B Meyer and P Olivier (eds), *Diagrammatic Representation and Reasoning*, Springer-Verlag (New York), 2001

Cassari, S (ed), *Peter Eisenman: Feints*, Skira (Milan), 2006

Clark, Roger H and Michael Pause, third edition, *Precedents in Architecture: Analytic Diagrams, Formative Ideas, and Partis*, John Wiley & Sons (Hoboken, NJ), 2005

Eisenman, P (introduction by RE Somol), *Diagram Diaries*, Thames & Hudson (London), 1999

Ferrater, B and C Ferrater, *Synchronising Geometry: Landscape Architecture and Construction/Ideographic Resources*, Actar (Barcelona), 2006

Harmon, KA, *You Are Here: Personal Geographies and Other Maps of the Imagination*, Princeton Architectural Press (New York), 2004

Ingold, T, *Lines: A Brief History*, Routledge (Oxford), 2007

Kim, Jong-Jin (ed), *Activity Diagrams*, Damdi Publishing (Seoul), 2006

Kostoff, S, *The City Shaped: Urban Patterns and Meanings Through History*, Thames & Hudson (London), 1999

Pai, H, *The Portfolio and the Diagram: Architecture, Discourse and Modernity in America*, MIT Press (Cambridge, MA), 2006

Reiser + Umemoto, *Atlas of Novel Tectonics*, Princeton Architectural Press (New York), 2006

Shane, DG, *Recombinant Urbanism: Conceptual Modeling In Architecture, Urban Design and City Theory*, Wiley–Academy, a division of John Wiley & Sons Ltd (Chichester), 2005

Stjernfelt, F, *Diagrammatology: An Investigation on the Borderlines of Phenomenology, Ontology, and Semiotics*, Springer (Dordrecht), 2007

Tufte, Edward R, *Envisioning Information*, Graphics Press (Cheshire, CT), 1990

Tufte, Edward R, *Visual Explanations: Images and Quantities, Evidence and Narrative*, Graphics Press (Cheshire, CT) 1997

Tufte, Edward R, *Visual and Statistical Thinking: Displays of Evidence for Making Decisions*, Graphics Press (Cheshire, CT), 1997

Tufte, Edward R, *The Visual Display of Quantitative Information* (Cheshire, CT), 2001

Tufte, Edward R, *Beautiful Evidence*, Graphics Press (Cheshire, CT), 2006

Journals

L Bijlsmer, Wouter Deen and Udo Garritzman (eds), *OASE: Diagrams* (Rotterdam), no 48, 1998

Ben van Berkel and Caroline Bos (eds), *ANY: Diagram Work* (New York), no 23, 1998

Gerrit Confurius (ed), *Daidalos: Diagrammania* (Berlin), no 74, January 2000

Fisuras: Diagramas (Madrid), vol 12.5, July 2002

Lotus International: Diagrams (Milan), no 127, 2006

David Dunster (ed), *Architectural Review*, January 2006

Index

Figures in italics indicate captions.